מסורה

ArtScroll Mesorah Series®

Expositions on Jewish liturgy, thought and Halachah

Rabbi Mordechai Gifter shlita

TORAH

Published by

Mesorah Publications, ltd

PERSPECTIVES

An eminent Rosh Yeshivah expounds on
such timely and timeless topics as
education, the Holocaust, and
the Jew's role in creation

FIRST EDITION
First Impression … September, 1986

Published and Distributed by
MESORAH PUBLICATIONS, Ltd.
Brooklyn, New York 11223

Distributed in Israel by
MESORAH MAFITZIM / J. GROSSMAN
Rechov Harav Uziel 117
Jerusalem, Israel

Distributed in Europe by
J. LEHMANN HEBREW BOOKSELLERS
20 Cambridge Terrace / Gateshead
Tyne and Wear / England NE8 1RP

ISBN
(Hard cover) 0-89906-228-8
(Paperback) 0-89906-229-6

Typography by CompuScribe at ArtScroll Studios, Ltd.
1969 Coney Island Avenue / Brooklyn, N.Y. 11223 / (718) 339-1700

Printed in the United States of America by Moriah Offset
Bound at Sefercraft, Brooklyn, NY

This volume is dedicated
to the memory of

Harav Israel Ehrenhaus זצ״ל

מוקדש לזכר נשמת

אאמו״ר הרה״ג

ר׳ ישראל אהרנהויז זצ״ל

He established a family tradition
of generosity and Torah support.
An admirer once described him in these words:

"The world has many happy folk
Who smile each day they live,
Because they've found that happiness
Depends on what you give.

For a giving man is different
From his neighbors in the pod;
When his thoughts are of his brothers,
Then he's closest to his G-d.

And the spark of love he kindles
In a breast where hope has died
Sheds a warmth that's like no other,
For it feels so good inside!

And every time he gives a bit
He adds a little part
To that something deep within him
That the poets call a heart."

Preface

The material presented in this booklet represents a collection of articles published in various journals and magazines during the past forty years. They deal with various topics in Jewish life. Their purpose was always to present a Torah perspective on Jewish problems, to see fact and events not merely through the human material eyes, but rather to view them through the spiritual sights of Torah.

The articles were originally published primarily in the Jewish Observer and Dos Yiddishe Vort of Agudath Israel and Jewish Parents Magazine of Torah Umesorah. I am very grateful to Rabbi Nosson Scherman for his translation of the articles originally published in Yiddish in Dos Yiddishe Vort.

I am most grateful to my dear friends Rabbis Meir Zlotowitz, Nosson Scherman, Sheah Brander and their wonderful staff for their devoted efforts in the publication of this book as befits the tradition of ArtScroll.

Looking forward to the advent of Mashiach Tzidkeinu Bimhera B'Yameinu.

Mordechai Gifter
Telshe

Table of Contents

A Word to Jewish Parents

The strongest and most significant factors in life happen to be those that are beyond the comprehension of the senses. Surely the soul is the source of human life, but no one has yet succeeded in perceiving this foundation of life with the five senses.

In the world of commandments as well, there are those that are the very soul of the other commandments. The essential physical act of *mitzvah* performance — the *act* that man performs with the aid of the senses — is the minimum requirement of the law. The commandments were given to us to cleanse, purify, and elevate human life — רָצָה הקב״ה לְזַכּוֹת אֶת יִשְׂרָאֵל לְפִיכָךְ הִרְבָּה לָהֶם תּוֹרָה וּמִצְוֹת , *The Holy One, Blessed is He, wished to purify Israel; therefore He gave them Torah and mitzvos in abundance (Makkos 23b)* — and it is this which represents the unimaginable power, the soul, of the commandment. The performance of commandments with a full awareness of the purpose and outcome of each one infuses the *mitzvah* with life, by means of which the person becomes invigorated and sanctified.

[Translated from *Dos Yiddishe Vort* of Nissan 5716/1956, this article provides Jewish parents a perspective on what their goals and ambitions should be for their children. — Ed.]

Because the power of a *mitzvah* is incomprehensible, there always exists the great danger of falsifying its content. A person must distill the holiness and life-spirit from the *mitzvah* — קִדְּשָׁנוּ בְּמִצְוֹתָיו, *He has sanctified us with His commandments* — but חַס וְשָׁלוֹם he dare not try to inject his *own* spirit into the *mitzvah*. A person must merge himself into the commandment, and not vice versa. And if the opposite does occur, G-d forbid, it is virtually inevitable that it will result in a heretical disbelief in the necessity of the *mitzvah* performance — in the tangible execution of the Divine command.

The Jew, therefore, always combines תּוֹרָה וּמִצְוֹת, *Torah and commandments*, in the same phrase. *Mitzvos* are always understood as a direct outcome of Torah, deriving their holiness and internal spiritual power from the utterance and will of *Hashem Yisborach*, which is revealed in the holy letters of our Torah. Regarding *mitzvos*, therefore, our Sages taught us, בִּזְמַן שֶׁהֵן עֲשׂוּיִין כְּמִצְוָתָן הֲרֵי הֵן מִצְוֹת, וּבִזְמַן שֶׁאֵין עֲשׂוּיִין כְּמִצְוָתָן אֵינָן מִצְוֹת, *When they are performed according to their commands, they are mitzvos, but when they are not performed according to their commands, they are not mitzvos.* And the only context of a *mitzvah* is its place within the letters of the Torah.

Such an approach and insight into the power and effectiveness of commandments requires of us a total and uncompromising dedication to Torah study. A profound understanding of the word of G-d as expressed in the letters of the Torah — only this can guide a person to a spiritually inspiring performance of the commandments. This is what our Sages taught in saying, וְלֹא עַם הָאָרֶץ חָסִיד, *an ignoramus cannot be scrupulously pious* (see the profound comment of *Rabbeinu Yonah* to *Avos* 2:5).

If real-life commandments must be "Torah *and* commandments," then we are compelled constantly to strive for higher and yet higher attainments in the world of Torah study and Torah greatness. There are many Jewish parents who want their children "to be devoutly observant Jews" but insist "he doesn't have to be a rabbi!" By this they mean to say that only a rabbi must spend years studying Torah. But such parents fail to understand the meaning of *mitzvah* performance.

Commandments sprout and develop in the rich soil of greatness in Torah. It is true that in Eastern Europe a large percentage of Jews was observant even though they were not great in Torah study. But we always forget the simple fact that the Jewish *community* — the entire complex of Jewish life — was led and directed by greatness in Torah. The Torah giants of the generation put their stamp on all of life, and the *mitzvah* performance of the ordinary Jew was planted in the rich soil of the generation's Torah greatness. Every household in Lithuanian Jewry knew about Reb Yitzchok Elchonon, Reb Chaim Brisker and the Chofetz Chaim ז״ל. The same was true of Polish or Hungarian Jewry with its great men. In such blessed soil, small bushes could flourish alongside the cedars of Lebanon, the powerful Torah figures of the generation.

In America, however, we have not yet succeeded in producing a tradition of greatness in the field of Torah study. We cannot be content, therefore, with raising merely "observant" children, "*mitzvah*" children. If Jewish parents wish to guarantee a truly Jewish life of *mitzvah* performance, they must expend the greatest possible effort and they must sacrifice to help create and fashion outstanding Torah personalities from among the American youth.

Even in a child's earliest years in *cheder* — here in America this stage is already glorified with the name *yeshivah*, and the more reticent call it *yeshivah ketanah* or elementary yeshivah — parents must already bear in mind the greatest goals. They must be inspired with an intense desire to see their son grow into a *gadol b'Torah*, a great Torah figure, whose personality will bespeak G-dly authority, who will stand tall and firm in his principles, and be gracious and yielding in his character attributes.

Let us not make the mistake of thinking that American young people do not possess the raw material of Torah greatness. That is false, completely false! We have among us, as well, the young genius who should become the *gaon*, the sage — we lack only the insight and the sense of colossal necessity to create *gedolim* and *geonim*. We understand the need for a Jonas Salk to combat the crippling effect of infantile paralysis, but we don't even begin to comprehend our need for the Torah giant who will combat the paralysis caused by superficiality in Jewish life. And because of this, we fail to respond to the most compelling needs of our time.

Our future *gedolim* often become lost to us because of the narrow-mindedness of parents, *observant* parents, who are so fearful over the material success of their children. We want devout children, but we are blind, *very* blind, to the simple truth that the *gaon*, the Torah giant, is the only guarantor of *mitzvah* performance. How low have we sunk if we can justify many years of higher yeshivah learning, of utter devotion to Torah, only in the light of — or better said, a strong ambition for — a livelihood in the rabbinate or Jewish education. Parents do not begin to understand that Torah study is a holy process of the Jewish personality's growth and development, independent of whatever material goal the student will eventually choose for himself, with G-d's help.

Due to the limited vision of American parents, the potential Torah giants of our time are being lost to us. And together with this enormous loss, we also lose the pure, Torah-inspired performance and observance of commandments of the entire community, because our *mitzvos* became empty and rote-like if they are torn from their root, the letters of the Torah.

Jewish parents, our religious parents, should think seriously: are they truly building the future of their children — or are they denying both themselves and their children?

Emunas Chachamim /
Faith in the Sages

In the month of Sivan, when we have celebrated *Shavuos*, the festival of the giving of the Torah, it is worthwhile for us to contemplate the teaching of the Sages, כַּמָּה טִפְּשָׁאֵי שְׁאָר אִינְשֵׁי דְקַיְמֵי מִקַּמֵּי סֵפֶר תּוֹרָה וְלֹא קַיְמֵי מִקַּמֵּי גַּבְרָא רַבָּה, *What fools are the people who stand in the presence of a Torah scroll, but do not stand in the presence of a Torah scholar (Makkos 22b).*

Torah can exist among the Jewish people only to the extent that the nation is capable of evaluating the Torah scholar, the *talmid chacham* whose very personality represents a Torah Presence. When it remains frozen in print, Torah can be lifeless and forlorn ח"ו — it *lives* only in the Jew whose soul is molded according to the Torah's rules and principles.

The Torah is unlimited in her depth and breadth: אֲרֻכָּה מֵאֶרֶץ מִדָּהּ וּרְחָבָה מִנִּי יָם, *Longer than the earth is its measure, and broader than the sea (Job 11:9)* — but she must have those who will strive to draw her life-giving waters and who will discover her wellsprings. The *talmid chacham* is the one who always uncovers new Torah horizons. In such a manner the impression is instilled that the Torah is not a sealed, limited

[The Rosh Yeshivah addresses a topic that goes against the grain of modern, secular man, but that is basic to Torah Judaism. From *Dos Yiddishe Vort*, Sivan 5716/1956. — Ed.]

presence; rather the very process of the giving of the Torah included the endless striving to bring it ever increasingly to human recognition. Consequently, Torah study is a constant continuation of the giving of the Torah — and generations after the Revelation at Sinai the *talmid chacham* can relive that moment through his learning, and his very being can proclaim: הַדְּבָרִים שְׂמֵחִים כִּנְתָנָתָן מִסִּינַי, *The words are as joyous as when they were given at Sinai.*

We dare not, however, make the mistake of thinking that all this happens simply through a mortal approach, as if we were approaching a human code of laws. In order to master a particular science, a person must first prepare himself to evaluate that science according to its unique characteristics. Good physicians are only those who approached medicine with a profound inner desire to study and master it. מִילְתָא אַלְבִּישַׁיְהוּ יַקִּירִי, *those who wear garments of precious wool can appreciate its value* (Shabbos 10b). If one wishes to master Torah wisdom, he must approach it according to the character of Torah wisdom, as the revelation of the Divine will. Our Sages teach us that just as the Torah was given through awe, fear and trembling — with a profound inner trembling and inspiration — so must the Torah be studied and expounded (*Berachos* 22a). Only then can it legitimately be called "Torah study," and only then can one hope to plumb a bit of its depth.

The Torah student who directs his life and study in the Torah path is the one who is crowned with the title *talmid chacham*. Torah Jewry sees in such scholars a continuation of the acceptance of the Torah through our teacher Moses. The *bais midrash* of such a *talmid chacham* represents the *bais midrash* of Moses, who receives the Torah from the Omnipotent (*Iggeres of R' Shmuel ben Eli*). Jewry does not see before itself a person who teaches his Torah to the generation; rather it observes the phenomenon of the Torah being presented to the Jewish nation through the agency of the *talmid chacham*. He serves as the river through which the Torah streams from the Creator to the Jewish nation.

And when we perceive the *talmid chacham* as the one who

upholds the unending, universal phenomenon of the Revelation at Sinai, in whom the Divine will is revealed to the Jewish nation, then we cannot but understand that when the Torah commands אֶת ה׳ אֱלֹקֶיךָ תִּירָא, *You are to fear HASHEM, your G-d*, then אֶת לְרַבּוֹת תַּלְמִידֵי חֲכָמִים, *the word* אֶת *comes to add Torah scholars* to the category of reverence for G-d *(Bava Kamma 41b)*.

From this deep conviction, Jews have derived the fundamental principle of *Emunas Chachamim*, faith in Torah sages: to believe in and be convinced in the correctness and consistency of the *daas Torah* of Israel's great men. Even when אוֹמְרִים לָךְ עַל יָמִין שֶׁהוּא שְׂמֹאל וְעַל שְׂמֹאל שֶׁהוּא יָמִין, *they tell you that right is left and that left is right*, when you feel that you understand better than they — and the truth is diametrically opposed to the Torah opinion of the *gedolei yisrael* — nevertheless לֹא תָסוּר מִן הַדָּבָר אֲשֶׁר יַגִּידוּ לְךָ, *you dare not turn away from whatever they tell you (Deuteronomy 17:11)*. This is not a matter of understanding a human being, this is a matter of understanding Torah, which is revealed to you by means of this person, this *talmid chacham*, this great Torah scholar. Woe to the generation that seeks right and left for the Torah to point the way, but that seeks it according to its own shrunken, human understanding instead of according to the wisdom of the Torah itself.

How far, how far is our generation from this life-principle of *Emunas Chachamim*! It is even possible for us not only to reject a ruling of the Torah leaders of the generation, but even to criticize it on the grounds that the *"gedolim* do not understand clearly the issue that they considered." And these critics bear the title "rabbi"! If the title "rabbi" contains any meaning at all, it lies in the fact that it represents the strength of the Torah. How empty, therefore, is a rabbinate that is devoid of *Emunas Chachamim*.

Without *Emunas Chachamim*, faith is lacking in the Principle of all principles, in *Hashem Yisborach* Himself! Without *Emunas Chachamim*, the entire concept of Torah's meaning to us is lacking. There is set forth a concept of Torah that is denuded of the revelation at Sinai. It is small wonder, therefore, that rabbis without *Emunas Chachamim* seek to fraternize with Conservative and Reform seducers and instigators; the entire concept of "right and left" has become perverted and corrupted — of knowing what is right and what is left. Whoever sees through Torah eyes becomes confounded by how possible it is for human logic to become the instrument of enormous perversity.

Isn't it time for people to consider, "What fools are the people ...?"

Daas Torah

Our Sages say, אָמַר רָבָא, לְמַיְמִינִין בָּה, סַמָּא דְחַיֵּי; לְמַשְׂמְאִילִים בָּה
סַמָּא דְמוֹתָא, *To those who go to the "right" with [the Torah], it is a potion of life; to those who go to the "left" with [the Torah], it is a potion of death (Shabbos 88a).* This means that the Torah *itself* acts as a potion of death to those who go to the left with it. *Rashi* explains that "going to the right" with it means: "they engage in it with all their strength, and are preoccupied with knowing its mystery, like someone who uses his right hand, which is his primary organ." From this we derive two important points: (1) What it means to be "engaged in Torah," i.e., "engaged with all their strength and preoccupied with it"; and (2) What the essence of Torah study is: "to know its mystery."

The meaning of "Torah's mystery" is not, as we are accustomed to say, that in the holy Torah there is a revealed portion and a hidden portion. Everything that a person is privileged to attain and understand of what he had previously not understood — this is the mystery of Torah. The very essence of Torah study is the revelation of mystery, to delve

[Basic to the acceptance of the Torah itself is the readiness to let it shape one's thought processes and guide his activities. From the *Shavuos Almanac* of *Dos Yiddishe Vort.* — Ed.]

ever more deeply into the depth of Torah. The same knowledge of Torah assumes a new dimension when one immerses himself into it more deeply. Whatever such a person has already attained through his intense effort becomes the simple meaning; and he plunges ahead, he plumbs more deeply, he reveals the unknown, the incomprehensible. He is always occupied in the revelation of mysteries.

So it is with the Written Torah and so it is with the Oral Torah. The young child begins studying "In the beginning G-d created" and has a childish understanding of Creation; but before he began to learn even that was a mystery, and his *rebbe* revealed the mystery. According to how much more the child develops himself in knowledge and understanding, the concept of Creation becomes clearer to him, and he reaches the level of development sufficient to find in the concept of Creation the idea that *Rashi* cites in his commentary to the first words of the Torah: Rabbi Yitzchok's teaching that the Torah related the order of Creation so that we would know that G-d created and allocates the world as He sees fit. As he grows, he sees more, and he finds in Rabbi Yitzchok what the *Ramban* teaches: that mortal man is incapable of understanding the process of Creation, but G-d wanted us to know that the course of history was fashioned by man's virtues and sins, and it was this process that led to the choice of Israel as G-d's people. As the child develops further in his wisdom, he delves more deeply and realizes, as *Targum Yerushalmi* teaches, that G-d created heaven and earth בְּחוּכְמָתָא, *with wisdom.*

This is a remarkable degree of advancement and development, with new insight at every level of development. And every insight reveals more, uncovers more; and the more that is revealed, the broader becomes his definition of simple meaning. The student begins to study *Gemara* and hears a s'vara, logical reasoning, from his *rebbe* — but at this stage of his maturity, the s'vara is but a "fact," the revelation of something he had not known before. He does not yet *feel* the s'vara intellectually, it is only a bare s'vara, unrelated to his entire reasoning process. Nevertheless he senses the revelation of a new world within Torah, the world of Torah logic. As he advances in learning, the very same s'vara assumes a new form. He has deciphered a mystery and transformed it to simple meaning, and his advancement expresses itself in his continuing to discover what was hidden, in feeling and appreciating the s'vara, in his entire being becoming enveloped by the intellectual adventure of understanding.

This is the essential nature of Torah study, to decipher the mystery of Torah.

The *Ramban*, in *Kuntres Emunah u'Vitachon*, teaches that there does not exist any portion of the mystical Torah that is divorced from the revealed portion — rather the mystical Torah is but the profundity of the revealed Torah. The entire holy Torah is a single entity, and learning consists of engrossing oneself in it, finding what is obscure, what is concealed.

This mystery of Torah extends all the way to G-d's own wisdom and will, and therefore there is no limit to the Torah's mysteries. The essential nature of Torah wisdom is not bounded by This World, and this is the basic difference between the Torah and all other intellectual pursuits. And for this reason Torah must be studied in a different manner than other kinds of knowledge. A discipline whose mystery, whose kernel of truth is limited must be studied with limitation. The discipline must be studied according to its nature. But the wisdom of the holy Torah is infinite and unbounded, so its study cannot tolerate limitation. Therefore, the human being who studies it must, as *Rashi* says, be engaged with all his strength and be preoccupied with it. Only so can Torah be studied. Consequently, *Rashi's* two conditions are in reality one.

Someone who studies Torah as if it were another discipline makes of it an ordinary subject, and when it is so relegated that it becomes a potion of death, the poison of the human spirit. Conversely, the one who studies Torah "with the right" is constantly bound and united with its mystery, with what he has *not yet* perceived, with what he does *not yet* understand. He is the wise man who draws the Torah's wisdom into actuality. But the one who goes to the *left* of the Torah is bound and united with the transitory and he draws the existence of the Torah towards his personal preferences.

The one who goes "to the left" with Torah searches in it for the logic-processes of other disciplines, and his efforts are in vain. He will find a Torah laden with contradictions. The basis of human thought is human logic, and in the Torah he will find the opposite of this logic. He will find שְׁנֵי כְתוּבִים הַמַּכְחִישִׁים זֶה אֶת זֶה, *two passages that contradict one another*, but he will not find the עַד שֶׁיָּבֹא הַכָּתוּב הַשְּׁלִישִׁי וְיַכְרִיעַ בֵּינֵיהֶם, *the third passage that comes to reconcile them*. He will see that the Torah forbids this and requires that, but his human logic will *not* understand the reconciliation that עֲשֵׂה דּוֹחֶה לֹא תַעֲשֶׂה, *a positive commandment overrides a negative commandment*. Before his eyes he will see an anachronistic welter of earlier and later, not realizing that the Torah is not written in chronological order (אֵין מוּקְדָּם וּמְאוּחָר בַּתּוֹרָה). And if, indeed, he is one of those who thinks, and as a result notices such contradictions in his human thought process, then ח״ו he will deny the Torah and the Giver of the Torah — and the Torah itself will have become his potion of death.

Whatever a person attains in Torah knowledge provides him with satisfaction in proportion to how much he regards it as bound up in the mystery he has not yet been privileged to reveal and uncover. אַשְׁרֵי הָאִישׁ ... כִּי אִם בְּתוֹרַת ה' חֶפְצוֹ וּבְתוֹרָתוֹ יֶהְגֶּה יוֹמָם וָלָיְלָה, *Praiseworthy is the man ... But his desire is in the Torah of* HASHEM, *and in his Torah he meditates day and night (Psalms 1:1-2)*. When his entire will, desire, and ambition are inextricably bound up with G-d's Torah — to the Torah that is still G-d's because it has not yet been revealed to human understanding — only then is he capable of sensing the infinite pleasure of his *own* Torah, which he has already succeeded in attaining. Every second, every minute during which someone lacks effort and struggle in Torah study, every minute that is free of struggle to master Torah — in that moment he is severed from the mystery of Torah and in that moment he has lost the pleasure of Torah.

From all of this we can infer of someone who goes to the right with Torah — לְמַיְמִינִין בָּהּ — that as a result of his constant bond with the mystery of the Torah, he has never dragged down to a human level what he has already accomplished, what he has come to understand of the Torah. Rather he has come to understand the Torah from its aspect of Divine mystery, the mystery of eternity, its aspect of G-d's will.

This is what we call *Daas Torah*, meaning that the judgment *(Daas)* of the person who studies is united with the mystery of the Torah. It is this *Daas Torah* that the great Torah figures of all generations were privileged to have. By means of this *Daas Torah*, the great men of Torah actually *see* what others, at best, *know* but do not *see*. The great Torah leaders are granted a "visual sense" from the world of the Torah's mystery, the world of eternity, at a time when smaller people understand and feel everything only according to our small world, the revealed world.

Woe to those who pose questions in the name of Torah — sincerely or insincerely — to the Torah greats, to the point where they ask, "Who appointed them *gedolim* that we must obey them?" Such people would reduce Torah authority to the miniscule dimension of an appointment or a position.

Not only do the Torah giants understand wisdom, they see deeply in wisdom, as King Solomon said וְלִבִּי רָאָה הַרְבֵּה חָכְמָה, *my heart saw much wisdom (Koheles 1:16)*.

Fortunate is the community and fortunate is the individual who "goes to the right with Torah." He will also be granted *Emunas Chachamim*, faith in the sages, to subject himself to the authority of the Torah giants and to conduct his life in accordance with *Daas Torah*.

(Adapted from the *Shiur Daas*, נִשְׁמַת הַתּוֹרָה)

The Function of Torah Chinuch
in Our Generation

◄§ Torah and Israel's Soul

The function of Torah *chinuch* is the creation of a society where Torah will not merely be one of a vast number of human interests but rather a society where all human interest, all human endeavor centers in and emanates from Torah. The proper function of Torah *chinuch*, therefore, is the development of an understanding and an appreciation of the nature of Torah and *mitzvos*.

Chazal (our Rabbis) long ago said: "The Holy One, blessed be He, wished to purify Israel, therefore did He give them much Torah and many *mitzvos*." It is taken for granted that without Torah there can be no *zakus hanefesh* — no purity of soul — for the human being is laden with the dross and alloy of earthly, sensory lusts and temptations. These tend to make of the human a beast, rather than the personification of the *tzelem Elokim* — a creature in the Divine image, a creature endowed with intellectual perception which makes it possible for him to see, observe and grasp things in a pure intellectual form, not subject to material sensory limitation.

["Jewish Education" is an acknowledged prerequisite of Jewish survival. But what is its purpose? What are the responsibilities of parents? The Rosh Yeshiva spoke on this theme to Torah Umesorah lay leaders. This digest of his address appeared in *The Jewish Parent*, June 1964. — Ed.]

This *zakus* — this purity — inheres within the soul of *Klal Yisrael*. In accepting Torah at Sinai, this became an inherent characteristic of the inner soul of our people. The halachah states that when a Jew is compelled by the *beis din* to perform any act which must be done under his own free will, such compulsion is considered free will because *mitzvah lishmo'a bedivrei chachamim* — it is a *mitzvah* to heed the instructions of the *bais din*. The *Rambam* explains the rationale of this *Halachah* as follows:

Compulsion refers only to an act in which there is no Torah obligation for performance. But a person who was overcome by his *yetzer hara* (evil inclinations) and was forced to commit a sin, whereupon *bais din* inflicted punishment as a restraint; this is not something forced upon him, but rather, to the contrary, it was he who forced himself to act improperly. This is so because as a Jew he wishes to be part of Israel and it is his desire to perform *mitzvos*. His *yetzer hara* has overwhelmed him. Since punishment was inflicted until the force of the *yetzer* subsided and he declared, "*Rotzeh ani* — I desire to perform the *mitzvah*," this then is an act of free volition not one of compulsion (*Hil. Gerushin* 2:20).

The inherent will and desire of the Jew is to be part of Israel and to live by Torah and *mitzvos*. *Yetzer hara* is an external influence which does not inhere in the soul of the Jew. Any compulsion to free the Jew of these external forces and motivations returns the Jew to his inherent self where naturally his will is Torah and *mitzvos*.

Our Rabbis noted this in their profound comment upon the words of *Koheles*, "*Vehanefesh lo timolei* — and the soul is never filled, never satisfied." It is like unto the royal princess who married a peasant. Whatever delicacies he prepared for her in his devotion never satisfied her for she was a royal princess. All the preparations of her husband lacked the one ingredient — *royalty*. *Nefesh Yisrael* (the soul of *Klal Yisrael*) — a portion of *malchus shamayim* (the Heavenly kingdom) — is wed unto the *guf* (the earthly material body of Man). All which this *guf* would do in satisfying the demands of the soul remains lacking in royal content, in the "princeliness" of Divinity. The inner self of the Jew consists of an unending thirst, a yearning for *kedushah*, for Divine sanctity and holiness. Our generation lacks peace of mind *(menuchas hanefesh)* because it is unaware of the nature of its restlessness. There is a yearning for Heaven which is fed with the food of Earth.

◄§ Torah Study in Depth

The basic, all-inclusive *mitzvah* of Torah is that of *emunah*, belief in the existence and Oneness of the Creator. This *mitzvah* was stated in the Ten Commandments in the words: *Anochi Hashem Elokecha.* This is a statement of fact, not the terminology of a commandment. This fact is the greatest Reality in Creation. And Reality obligates and commands. It commands the profound reflection, meditation and contemplation necessary to invest ourselves with the feeling and recognition of this Reality.

In his *Yad*, the *Rambam* discusses the profound contemplation of *emunah*. He devotes to it four chapters which represent the quintessence of Jewish religious philosophy. At the very end of his discussion, he postulates that these profound philosophic considerations can be of value and content only if they stem from and are based upon the strong foundations of *lechem u'bosor* — the bread and meat of *havayos d'Abaya v'Ravah* — the deep study of Torah in expounding the *mitzvas Hashem*, because these *havayos d'Abaya v'Ravah* serve to regulate and discipline the thinking process of the human mind. The strength of mind, the intellectual force, necessary for the profound philosophic consideration of *emunah* are achieved only through the depths of Torah study.

The inherent qualities of the Jew, with which he is endowed to reach the heights of the Supreme Reality of *emunah*, these qualities are activated to become a practical force through the study of Torah as the prerequisite in *shmiras hamitzvos* — in the observance and performance of *mitzvos*.

Torah *chinuch*, then, is the "bread and meat" of *havayos d'Abaya v'Ravah*.

⁊ Total Engrossment in Study of Torah

These *havayos d'Abaye v'Ravah* are endowed with their own specific characteristic, unique to the study of Torah. Our Rabbis teach us: "*Im bechukosai teileichu* — if you shall walk in My statutes — *shetiheyu ameilim ba-Torah* — if you shall *labor* in Torah!" This concept of *amal haTorah* is inherent to the study of Torah. *Amal haTorah* means the complete engrossment of the student in Torah to the exclusion of all else. It means a mind completely open to Torah, unburdened with other systems of thought. It means a self-denial of material interests and desires. It signifies the power and ability to find in Torah study all the joy and pleasure which one could wish for. It means finding in Torah the joys and benefits "of bread and meat, of wine and oil, of fields and vineyards, of milk and honey, of precious stones and pearls."

Amal haTorah does not mean a life impoverished by complete removal from human joys and pleasures but rather the sublime contentment of the most intimate contact with the source of all joy and pleasure.

This is the content of the two *berachos* recited daily upon the study of Torah. One, *la'asok b'divrei Torah* — not merely to study Torah, but that study become an *esek* — a complete involvement. The second *berachah*, *veha'arev na* (let it be pleasant), helps us find the *mesikus haTorah* — the sweetness of Torah.

Amal haTorah — this unique characteristic of Torah study creates a unique world for the Torah student. His greatest sorrow is the *kushya* — a difficult passage which he cannot master, a difficult *Rambam* attacked by the critique of a *Ra'avad*. The greatest joy of the Torah student is the *terutz* — he has seen the light, he has felt the truth and with the Psalmist he sings forth: "Unveil my eyes and I shall see the sublime wonders of Your Torah."

The *Halachah* states that if a student of Torah should have to be sentenced to exile, it is the duty of the *bais din* to exile the *Rav* with him. For in reference to *galus* it is written "and he shall live" — do all necessary to give him life and sustenance and the *Rambam* comments: "For the students of Torah, life without Torah study is considered death."

This is what the Jew means when he says of Torah: *Ki heim chayeinu v'orech yameinu"* — they are our life, and length of our days.

◂§ Striving in Torah Leads to Faith

This concept of Torah study is inherent to the concept of *shemiras hamitzvos*. The observance of *mitzvos* stems from *amal haTorah*. Otherwise, it becomes perfunctory, void of inner content.

The Torah teaches that the Almighty is *oseh chessed l'ohavoi u'leshomrei mitzvosoi* — He showers His loving kindness upon those who love Him and those who observe His *mitzvos*. And the Rabbis comment: *Shomrei mitzvosoi — eilu zekenim u'nevi'im*. Observant Jews are the *zekenim* — the *gedolei haTorah* and the prophets of the generations. The observance of *mitzvos* is predicated upon the *gadol baTorah*.

This process of Torah study starts at the earliest possible age: *Tinok sheyachol ledaber, Aviv melamdo Torah* — as soon as a child is able to speak, it is incumbent upon his father to teach him Torah. This precious faculty of speech is not to be wasted upon foolishness. It must, from the very beginning, be dedicated to Torah.

What is the first lesson taught to the Jewish child? *Torah tzivah lanu Moshe morashah kehilas Yaakov* — the complete Torah, the Written and Oral Law, was handed down to us as our heritage. And with it the *Shema* — the supreme Reality of *emunah*. The eternal heritage of Torah study, the basis for *emunah*, is the first Torah lesson taught to the Jewish child.

This heritage of Torah, the perpetuity of Torah in *Klal Yisrael* is predicated upon the concept of *amal haTorah*. The study of the word of Torah must be performed in the original form of its acceptance at Sinai. The act of Torah study must reflect the *Ma'amad Har Sinai*. Just as Torah was given at Sinai with an inner trembling, with a complete shattering of normal composure, so also must it be studied and taught.

We finite beings do not possess the faculties to encompass Torah, the wisdom of Infinity. The teacher or student of Torah, through the process of *amal haTorah*, can but purify himself, to create and make of himself a receptacle in which *Hashem* in His Divine Mercy implants Torah. This is the content of the third *berachah* daily upon Torah: *Vechayei olam nota besochainu*. He has implanted within us the eternal life of Torah.

Rambam points out that the eternal authority of Torah rests upon our ability to transmit from generation to generation not only the word of Torah but the *Ma'amad Har Sinai* which we witnessed and personally perceived. We are commanded not to forget any particular of that world-shattering event. Torah reached all of *Klal Yisroel*, not through the medium of *Moshe Rabbeinu*, but directly from *Hashem*. We heard it with our own ears, we saw it with our own eyes. We therefore know, out of personal experience and perception, the truth of Torah for all time. We will therefore deny and contradict with full force anyone who attempts to raise doubts in the truth of Torah.

⊷§ Our Task Today

Torah *chinuch* means that parents bear testimony to their children: Hear my child, I am witness to the fact that G-d gave us a Torah. So did I hear, so did I see! This, my child, is our heritage. I am not telling you Bible stories. I am relating the greatest singular event in the history of Mankind which I personally witnessed at Sinai.

We must measure success or failure in the light of *zakus hanefesh*. How far have we gone towards changing the consciousness of our generation? How far have we gone towards making *amal haTorah* the generating force of Jewish living? How far have we gone towards creating *zekenim* — *Gedolei Torah*? Ours is a day of specialization. How far have we gone towards implanting into the young minds and hearts of Day School children the dream of becoming a *Torah specialist?* How many of them dream of becoming a *Chofetz Chaim,* a *Reb Chaim Brisker,* a *Reb Meir Simchah,* a *Chazon Ish?*

Much indeed has been achieved in the past two decades. But with the great change that has been wrought we have not *yet* brought this generation to Sinai. We have not made this generation see what was seen, and hear what was heard.

The challenge of Torah *chinuch* is that "we come close to the mountain" and that we take our children with us to see and hear what our forefathers saw and heard. We must become witness to the great Reality of *emunah,* with renewed intensive efforts in consolidating positions already won, and in the continued conquest of new horizons for Torah.

The Philosophy and Structure
of the Midos Program

ᴥ§ Introduction

Permit me to preface my remarks with a paraphrase of Rabbi
Moshe Chayim Luzatto, z"l, in his introduction to his classic
work on ethics and morals, *Mesilas Yesharim* (The Path of the
Upright):

"I do not intend to say here what you do not know, but
rather to remind you of what is already known and very
evident. For most of what I will say are things which most
people know, and concerning which they entertain no doubts.
But to the extent that they are well known and their truths
revealed to all, so is forgetfulness in relation to them extremely
prevalent. It follows then that any benefit to be obtained from
these remarks is not to be derived from hearing them but once,
for most likely you will feel that you have learned little, after
hearing, that you did not know before. Its benefit is to be
derived, rather, through review and persistent study, by which
one is reminded of those things which, by nature, he is prone to
forget and through which he will take to heart the obligation
that he tends to overlook" (Preface, *Mesilas Yesharim*).

[The Samuel A. Fryer Educational Research Foundation was founded to
explore ways to improve and strengthen the *middos* (ethics) program of
Torah Umesorah affiliated day schools. The Rosh Yeshivah delivered the
Foundation's first annual lecture at a conclave held in April 1967. — Ed.]

✥ Israel and the Nations of the World

To do justice to the ideal for which the Samuel A. Fryer Ethics Foundation has been established, we must at the very outset clarify to ourselves that we intend to deal with *mussar* and *midos* (ethics and morals) from the vantage point of Torah. We must be conscious of the fact that when the Jew says: "He Who has made a distinction between light and darkness, between Israel and the nations" (Havdalah service), he thereby declares the similarity of these two distinctions. "Light and darkness" are not differences in degree but rather in kind; there is no point of contact between the two. "Israel and the nations" also represents a difference in kind, not in degree. Israel's approach to all problems is that of Torah and Torah alone. The approach of "the nations" rests upon totally different foundations.

This basic distinction is indicated in the uniqueness of wording found in the recitation of the blessings pertaining to *chachmah* — wisdom. The *Halachah* (Law) states that upon seeing a *chacham* (scholar, sage) from the nations of the world, one is to recite the blessing "Who has given of His wisdom to flesh and blood." Upon seeing a *chacham* of Israel, one of the scholars of the Torah, we recite the blessing, "Who has apportioned of His wisdom to those who revere Him." The wisdom of the Torah is in essence never totally disassociated from its Source — its Divine Donor; it is always a part of *Hashem*, because the Torah scholar is in essence never disassociated from the Almighty — "for His people are part of Him" *(Deuteronomy 32:9)*. This concept of *chachmah*, and *chachamim* in Torah is defined in the term *y'reiov* (those who revere Him), as different from *basar v'dam (flesh and blood)* *(Taz, Orach Chayim 224:6)*.

The Mishnah (Oral Law), as you know, has a treatise devoted specifically to the problems with which the Fryer Foundation intends to deal. It is *Maseches Avos — Pirkei Avos*. The introductory *Mishnah* to *Avos* is: "Moses received the Torah at Sinai and transmitted it to Joshua" *(Mishnah, Avos*

I:1). It is the only reference to *Seder Hamesorah*, the order of the Oral Tradition, in all of *Torah SheB'al Peh* (Oral Law). We should stop to think why this *Mishnah* was not placed as an introduction to *Berochos*, the first tractate in the Six Orders of the Mishnah. The *Bertenora* points out:

"This Tractate is not based on a commandment of the Torah as are other Tractates; rather, it deals completely with ethics and morals."

All of the Oral Law deals with the *mitzvos* of *Toras Hashem* (G-d's Torah); and it is to be assumed that the student of Torah is one who is conscious of the fact that he is studying G-d's Torah, not a humanly devised system of law. However, *Maseches Avos* deals with *mussar* and *midos*, with the problems of human ethics and morals.

"Non-Jewish scholars have also created works, brought forth from their human, intellectual resources, dealing with the problems of ethical behavior, to determine the conduct of man toward his fellow-man" (Bertenora, *Avos* I:1).

Therefore *Avos* has been introduced with a *Mishnah* pertaining to the source of Torah, the receiving of the Torah at Sinai, to teach us that the ethics and morals discussed in *Avos* are not the product of human intellectual endeavor, attained by the Sages, but that these principles of ethics are also Torah from Sinai (ibid.).

We may take note of a few instances to clarify what the *Bertenora* teaches us.

◂§ Torah Ethics

1. One of the character traits of the Jewish people is that of *bayshonus* — bashfulness. This inherent trait is a determining factor in much of the conduct of the Jew. Whence does it stem? What is the source of the Jew's bashfulness? Our *Chazal* (Sages) teach us: "so that the fear of G-d be impressed upon your face, so that you shall not sin" (*Exodus* 20:17, *Yevamos* 79a).

The bashfulness of the Jew is the identification mark of *yiras shomayim* (fear of *Hashem*). It signifies his inherent consciousness of imperfection before G-d, giving him a sense, a feeling of shame.

Ours is an age void of G-d-awareness and G-d-consciousness. It is therefore a generation which knows no shame. Thus, the inherent character barrier against crime and violence is lost. Small wonder, therefore, that ours is an age of moral decay and perversion.

2. The Torah relates that Pharaoh issued a decree to drown all (Jewish) male children at birth. The Torah teaches:

"The midwives, Shifrah and Puah, feared G-d and did not, therefore, do as Pharaoh had decreed" (Exodus 1:17).

What can make of man a moral being? What will determine his conduct in a moment of crisis? No humanly designed code of ethical conduct can do so. Fear of G-d is the governing factor in molding the character of man. The truth of this lesson was taught so poignantly when the Kulter Volk became the beast of the Hitler holocaust.

3. Let us remind ourselves of the episode of Joseph and the wife of Potiphar — that critical moment in the drama of Joseph which bestowed upon him, for eternity, the title of Tzaddik (the righteous one) (Genesis 39:7-16). What was it which turned Joseph into Yoseph HaTzaddik? In his attempt to prevail upon Potiphar's wife, he sought to impress upon her the fact that he had been entrusted with great responsibility by Potiphar, her husband. To acquiesce to her wishes would therefore be a breach of faith and trust. His appeal, then, was one of ethical conduct and behavior. But he added, "How then, can I do this great wickedness, and sin against G-d?" (Genesis 39:9).

◄§ Source of Ethical Conduct

Ethical conduct is void of content if it does not stem from the fear of G-d. It is this fear of G-d which is the motivating force of moral and ethical conduct in human affairs. When this motivation is removed, society becomes permeated with the lusts, the temptations, and the forms of vice prevalent today. To flee from reality in the hallucinations of LSD becomes part of the cultural milieu of modern society. The element of *chatasi l'Elokim* (I have sinned toward G-d) converts the lust and urge to sin into an insatiable thirst for holiness.

David, King of Israel, said, "I set the L-rd before me at all times." The *Ramah*, in the opening paragraph of the *Shulchan Aruch Orach Chayim* quotes Maimonides in interpreting what these words mean:

> We do not sit, move, and occupy ourselves, when we are alone and at home, in the same manner as we do in the presence of a great king. We speak and open our mouths as we please when we are with the people of our own household and with our close ones, but not so when we are in a royal assembly. We must awaken from our sleep and bear in mind that the Great King Who is over us, and is always joined to us, is greater than any earthly king. He always looks down upon us, beholding us and watching us, as the prophet Jeremiah says (23:24): 'Can anyone hide himself in secret places that I shall not see him?' (*Orach Chayim* 1:1)

When a person bears this in mind, he will be filled with the fear of G-d, with humility and piety, and with true, not merely surface, reverence and respect of G-d. Then will his conduct, even when alone, be the same as when in public intercourse with other people. Our Sages thereupon said: "Who is truly possessed of humility? He whose conduct in the dark night is the same as in the day" (*Moreh Nevuchim* 3:52).

This then is the basic Torah approach to ethical conduct. It is predicated upon and grows forth from an everpresent G-d-consciousness.

The ideal Torah life has been defined by Abba Shaul:

"*Zeh Keyli v'anveihu — hevei domeh lo*" (*Shabbos* 133b). ("This is my G-d and I will glorify Him — Be like unto Him"). And *Rashi* comments: "*Anveihu — ani v'hu — e'eseh atzmi k'moso*" ("I and He — I will make myself to be like Him"). The word *anveihu* (I will glorify Him) defines the Torah personality. It is the person in whom G-d is seen. "Just as He is merciful and kind, so shall you be merciful and kind" (ibid.).

The word *anveihu*, as explained by *Rashi* in the commentary to *Chumash*, means also *noy* (beauty). Man represents sublime beauty when there emanates from him G-dliness, that divine light which sublimates earthliness, and makes a man a *tzelem Elokim* — the image of the L-rd. This is the royal dignity of man.

⊷ The Practice of Ethics

This is the ideal, but no ideal can be achieved if it is not vested in the concrete form of practice in a *mitzvah ma'asis* (a practical *mitzvah*). No spiritual ideal is of value if it is not experienced materially through the practice of *mitzvah*. Without the practical *mitzvah* the ideal remains a matter of theory alone with little effect upon the conduct and behavior of man.

The ideal, therefore, of *anveihu — ani v'hu —* (I will glorify Him — I and He) so totally and all-embracing has been given concrete form in one of the 613 *mitzvos; that mitzvah* is: "And you shall walk in His ways" *(Deuteronomy* 28:9), which means that we are to act in our behavior and conduct and thought in a manner like unto that way in which G-d reveals Himself to man.

"Just as He is called merciful — mercy being an attribute of the Deity — so shall you be merciful. Just as He is called holy — holiness being an attribute of G-d — so shall you be holy."

The purpose of the attributes used in reference to the Deity is: "to teach us that these are good and just rules of conduct, since they are Divine in essence, and it is, therefore, incumbent upon us that we train ourselves in this way to be like unto Him to the best of our human ability" *(Maimonides, Deos* I:6).

The prophet Jeremiah says, "So says G-d: 'Let not the wise man glory in his wisdom, the mighty man in his might, nor the rich man in his riches' " *(Jeremiah* 9:22).

Chachmah (wisdom) in this passage is explained by Maimonides as referring to moral and ethical perfection, the highest degree of excellency in man's character. Most of the *mitzvos* aim at this perfection. However, all moral principles concern the relation of man to his fellow-man; the perfection of moral and ethical principles is, as it were, given to man for the benefit of mankind.

Imagine a person being alone and having no contact whatever with any other person; all his moral principles are at rest, they are not required and give man no perfection whatsoever. They are necessary and useful only when man is in contact with others.

The prophet Jeremiah continues: "Let man glory in this, that he understands and knows Me" *(Jeremiah* 9:23). This then is true perfection: The possession of the highest intellectual faculties used in the perception of G-d. In this, man attains his final objective, a perfection which remains within him alone, giving him immortality, and on its account he is called man.

The prophet continues: "For I am the L-rd Who does loving-kindness, justice and righteousness, for in these things I delight" (ibid.). Says Maimonides: "Full knowledge of G-d is, indeed, the final objective of man, and moral perfection is not the final objective, but yet this *haskel ve'yodeah* (knowledge of G-d) must again be translated into the sphere of the moral act. Having acquired knowledge of G-d, he will then be determined always to seek loving-kindness, justice, and righteousness, and thus to imitate the ways of G-d" *(Moreh Nevuchim* 3:54).

Moral and ethical conduct and practice are not to be viewed as ends in themselves, but rather as the *investiture in practice* of the final objective in human perfection — communion with G-d.

All of the foregoing has been expressed concisely by the Torah itself:

"And now, Israel, what does the L-rd, your G-d ask of you, but to walk in all His ways, to Love Him and serve the L-rd, your G-d, with all your heart and all your soul, to observe the *mitzvos* of G-d and all His statutes" *(Deuteronomy* 10:12,13).

Here the Torah has stated the totality of Jewish living, the total commitment of the Torah Jew. Walking in His ways, as we have seen, embodies the whole area of cultivation and correction of character traits. The essence of this concept of "walking in His Ways" is that a person conform all of his traits and all his various actions to what is just and ethical; that is, all that he does leads to the end of true good, namely, strengthening of Torah and furthering of the human fraternity (Introduction, *Mesilas Yesharim*).

Ethical living derives from the knowledge and fear of the L-rd and is expressed in the practice of conduct similar to that of G-d, designed to make a person one who loves G-d and serves Him in total commitment to the observance of all His *mitzvos*.

◆§ The Program in the School

All that has been said here must be made part of the school and the classroom.

Ethical and moral perfection, we are told by Rabbeinu Yonah, calls for three prerequisites. These are: (1) An environment conducive to proper Torah living; (2) personal fear of Heaven; (3) the study of Torah with a deep appreciation of and love for such study (commentary on *Proverbs* 1:8).

◆§ Midos Program

In the frame of reference of the elementary Torah school, this means that both the administration and the teaching staff must, themselves, be fully conscious of the ethical ideal, for they are primarily responsible for creating a school atmosphere — a *ruach* — conducive to developing in the young child a natural feeling for the moral and the ethical. Their manner of living should represent *yiras shamayim* (fear of Heaven) to the best of their ability. They must be fully aware of the fact that they are not merely teachers of subject matter but rather the spiritual parents of the children entrusted to them. Their responsibility is that of *mevio lidei chayei olam haba*, bringing the child into the life of "the world to come" *(Bava Metzia 33a).* The entire relationship of pupil to teacher, in the Torah outlook, is built upon this foundation. The school is then to the child not merely a *beis hasefer* (a school), but much more than that, it is a *beis hachinuch* (a house of education) — the house where the personality of the child is molded and developed. This is the essence of that term for elementary education unique to Torah education, *tinokos shel beis rabban* (the children of the house of their master).

A vital factor in this *beis chinuch* for these *tinokos shel beis raban* is the development of a sense of appreciation of authority. Ethical and moral living is *disciplined living*. It is the discipline of *kovesh es yitzro* — the strength to subdue, to exercise control over natural inclinations. Just as an undisciplined society is anarchy, so also is the undisciplined individual an example of anarchy in that great complex of desires, inclinations, urges, drives and emotions which are man.

Guided by the discipline of authority, the fear of and reverence for his teacher, the child must be led into the authority of G-d — the fear of Heaven. A love for the study of Torah, coupled with a willingness to sacrifice for it, must emerge from this guided discipline — the third prerequisite of Rabbeinu Yonah. The study of Torah, in the proper manner, is the greatest single factor in creating the moral and ethical personality of the Torah Jew.

When Torah is taught and studied through an awareness of the principle, *Torah min Hashamayim* (Torah is from Heaven), the teacher becomes an instrument through which G-d speaks to the child. *Ko amar Hashem* (so said G-d) is not something of the past. It is being said *this very moment* to the child. Can there be anything more conducive to morals and ethics than contact with the very Source of holiness? Can there be any greater inducement to compassion than contact with Him who is the very Source of compassion, of mercy, of every ethical principle in life. This, indeed, is Torah study when properly given to the child.

We would be remiss in thinking that a *midos* program for *tinokos shel beis rabban* involves just research in the subject matter of ethics and morals. What it really means is a full appraisal of our understanding of the purpose and intent of *tinokos shel beis rabban*. Such an appraisal, or reappraisal, will among other things also lead us to methods and formulae in conveying to the pupil specific training in specific areas of *midos*, of character and personality development. I say formulae, for there can be no *one* set formula in character training.

"Not all people are alike; not all places nor all times are the same." So said that giant of ethical perfection, Rabbi Yisrael Salanter. In the development of character we are dealing with the soul of the individuals. *Lokeach nefashos chacham* — to capture the soul is an act of great wisdom. If we shall set for ourselves the task of appraising our overall purpose in the context of "the children who learn (Torah)," the Almighty will help us find the road to the heart of the child entrusted to us so that ultimately it will become *chacham lev yikach mitzvos* — a heart perfected in the wisdom of ethical and moral living and yearning to express itself in the commandment of G-d."

The Dual Nature of Man

The world of the yeshivah student is that of the ד׳ אַמּוֹת שֶׁל הֲלָכָה, the four ells of the *Halachah.* In the vast expanse of the cosmos these four ells seem to be very confined. The life, therefore, of the *ben yeshivah* is usually viewed as a very cloistered life. The yeshivah student is looked upon as one who is removed from the mainstream of living. And the question is asked: "What does the *ben yeshivah* contribute to life?"

This constitutes the attitude not only towards the yeshivah student but, on a broader scale, the attitude of the secular Jew to the Torah Jew. And, therefore, in seeking to understand the world of the yeshivah we seek, in a sense, to understand the world of the Torah Jew and to place it in its proper perspective.

It must become clear to us that Man is a dual personality; עָפָר מִן הָאֲדָמָה, dust of the earth, limited and temporal; and נִשְׁמַת חַיִּים, the living soul, hewn from the infinite and eternal Being of Almighty G-d. *Dust of the earth* has reference not merely to the flesh and bones, the bodily structure of Man. It has reference to all in the human personality which is identi-

---

[The Rosh Yeshiva calls upon us to ponder whether the study hall is a cloistered enclave or the life-force of the cosmos. And he gives us the grounds to decide. From *The Jewish Observer,* January 1966. — Ed.]

fied with earthliness, all that is temporal in essence and nature. It refers to the character traits embedded in human nature which are ignoble and tend to corrupt the human personality. And *the living soul* has reference to all in the human personality which is divine in essence and makes possible to see in Man a צֶלֶם אֱלֹקִים, a creature in the Divine image.

This duality in Man places him in a unique position in the entire plan of Creation. Harmony in this duality is the gift of creativity with which Man has been endowed. The entire world has been placed at his disposal, כֹּל שַׁתָּה תַחַת רַגְלָיו, *all have You placed beneath his feet* — said King David (Psalms 8:7). When he was brought forth, his Creator commanded him: כִּבְשׁוּהָ, *subdue the earth.* If Man was so commanded he was endowed with the power and capacity to effect such rule. But long ago the Sages pointed out that the Torah uses advisedly the word רְדוּ (which can be translated both as *rule* and as *descend*) when referring to the rule of Man over the creatures of the world. If Man uses his powers properly he rules, but if he uses this power improperly then רְדוּ, descend, leave the heights of Creation for which you were chosen and ordained.

To subdue the world from the vantage point of *guf* (body) results in the despot who is ultimately destroyed by his own handiwork. To subdue from the vantage point of *neshamah* (soul) results in the great act of creativity, sublimation of an earthly temporal existence to its original primary source. In this process of subjugation Man sublimates himself.

However, no human achievement, no matter how sublime, is completely valid if it is not translated into *guf.* Such was the Divine Will and Wisdom of the Creator. Every human achievement must be realized by the entire personality of Man. When lived by the complete person then it is a complete achievement. This is the unique nature and mystery of the human personality. And, therefore, in the language of the Torah, the communion of Man with G-d, the most sublime of all human experiences, is the language of the mundane temporal world — וַיֶּחֱזוּ אֶת הָאֱלֹקִים וַיֹּאכְלוּ וַיִּשְׁתּוּ, They observed G-d, and they ate and drank (Exodus 24:11).

Throughout history Man has been thrust forward in world dominion by endless drives and urges which know no bounds. Long ago did King Solomon say: *He who loved worldly riches is never satiated with these riches (Koheles 5:9)*. And the Sages said: *He who has one manah desires two.* Every achievement serves as an impulse to new gains, but from whence stems this endlessness? The Sages said: *He who loves the mitzvah is not satiated by the mitzvah*, the primary source of these endless drives in human nature is rooted in *neshamah*, the love of *mitzvah*; fulfilling G-d's will, knows no bounds. Man has taken these drives, this insatiable urge of *mitzvah* and translated it into *guf*. This is as it should be. But in the process translation has become conversion. He has forgotten the primary source of these propulsion jets of human achievement. And we have Man declaring, *My power and the strength of my hand have made for me this great success (Deuteronomy 8:17)*. We have the cosmonaut, intoxicated with the nectar of achievement, declaring there is no G-d, ח"ו, for he has not encountered Him in his adventures in the vast expanse of outer space.

We must be careful to observe that we do not speak here of religion and secularism. Religion is also *guf* centered. The Sages pointed this out long ago when they commented upon the words of Torah: וּפַרְעֹה חֹלֵם וְהִנֵּה עֹמֵד עַל הַיְאֹר, *and Pharaoh was dreaming, and behold! he was standing over the river (Genesis 41:1)*. The Nile River was a deity in Egypt, yet Pharaoh stood *over* it. Upon this the Sages expound: The nations of the world stand above their gods, but the Jews have their G-d standing above them.

◄§ "When They Need Gold"

In reference to Pharaoh and his ilk, part of the needs of Man are his spiritual needs. He needs religion, he needs a synagogue. And just as he uses material things for *guf*, so also does he use spiritual values for *guf*. His religion is also utilitarian. The Sages said in commenting on the two phrases,

אֱלֹהֵי כֶסֶף וֵאלֹהֵי זָהָב, *gods of silver and gods of gold*, and וֵאלֹהֵי מַסֵּכָה, *gods of molten metal:*

When they need their gold for material purposes they make their idols of silver and when they need their silver, they make their gods of molten metal.

Guf is the assertion of one's self. And the human personality finds need to assert itself in matters of the spirit. This is not *neshamah*, for *neshamah* is the denial of self in the presence of the Supreme Being.

Guf feels itself as a whole entity. *Neshamah* recognizes itself as a fragment of the Creator. From *neshamah* there stems ענוה (humility), the feeling of human inadequacy which urges, which drives man to the recognition that the only true "I" is אנכי ה' אלקיך, *I am the L-rd your G-d* — the commandment of Faith, of אמונה.

Mesorah — tradition — is the basis of Torah and Torah life. The Mishnah in *Avos* lays down the postulate of *Mesorah* as the prerequisite for the righteous moral and ethical norm of life. *Guf* lives within the present fleeting moment, temporal in nature. *Neshamah* is eternal, part of an endless past and an endless future. The study of Torah and the life of *mitzvah* invests the Jew with the sublimation of *neshamah*. The mundane and secular becomes holy. Life becomes blessed with the spark of Divinity. Was this not what the Sages meant when they said in the Mishnah (*Makkos* 23b): רָצָה הקב"ה לְזַכּוֹת אֶת יִשְׂרָאֵל לְפִיכָךְ הִרְבָּה לָהֶם תּוֹרָה וּמִצְוֹת, *The Holy One, Blessed is He, wished to purify Israel, and therefore did He give them much Torah and many mitzvos.* Maimonides explains this to mean that in such a vast array of six hundred and thirteen *mitzvos* an individual is bound to find one *mitzvah* in which he is able to sublimate himself, to perform the *mitzvah* without regard for mundane interests, and thereby find G-d. And from this spark of Divinity all of life will be illuminated with *neshamah* and Man becomes part of eternity.

The human in his very being is an incomplete entity, part of the whole of *Hashem Yisborach*. Torah, the revelation to Man of G-d's Will, is therefore of necessity given to Man in incomplete form, only as a part, as a portion of His Divine Wisdom. The greatest act of communion with G-d, therefore, is incomplete Man driven to achieve completeness, something which he can find only in the one true and complete entity, the Supreme Being. The means of achieving this communion in its highest form is the union of Man's intellect with the Divine intellect revealed in Torah. The study of Torah is therefore, in a sense, synonymous with the experience of נבואה, of prophecy. So have we been taught by the Sages (*Bava Basra* 12a): מִיּוֹם שֶׁחָרַב בֵּית הַמִּקְדָּשׁ, אַף עַל פִּי שֶׁנִּטְלָה נְבוּאָה מִן הַנְּבִיאִים, מִן הַחֲכָמִים לֹא נִטְלָה, *Since the Beis Hamikdash was destroyed, even though prophecy was removed from the prophets, it was not removed from the Torah sages.* The prophetic experience is born of the never ceasing urge of *neshamah,* that incomplete portion of Divinity in Man — which yearns to find completeness. This is what *Koheles* referred to when he said: וְהַנֶּפֶשׁ לֹא תִּמָּלֵא, and the soul is not fulfilled.

This incompleteness of *neshamah* which experiences the joy of fullness only in G-d is the source for the strength of *Klal Yisrael — Knesses Yisrael.* Every individual is merely a portion of the whole and, therefore, one Jew is integrally associated with his fellow Jew. Complete entities can be dissociated from one another. Incomplete entities find themselves in unity with each other through their unity with the one G-d of Whom their *neshamos* have been hewn. This is the bedrock of Jewish communal responsibility unique to *Klal Yisrael,* enunciated in the maxim: *All Israel is responsible one to the other.*

◄§ An Attitude Toward Life

In realizing that the wholesomeness of a full life is achieved only in G-dly communion, something which is never completed in our mundane life, the Jew develops an attitude toward life which gives him the courage and fortitude to overcome trial and travail. That which in the mundane world is a source for sorrow and pain will in the future be experienced as the same act of G-d's kindness and compassion, as those life experiences which are now a source of joy and satisfaction. So we are taught by the Mishnah: *For all those experiences over which we must today recite the blessing reserved for sorrow* (בָּרוּךְ ... דַּיָן הָאֱמֶת), *in the future for these very same experiences we shall recite the blessing designated for occasions of joy* (בָּרוּךְ ... הַטוֹב וְהַמֵּטִיב).

This duality, the mundane and temporal, side by side with the Divine and the Eternal, therein lies the glory of Man as the chosen one of Creation. Perhaps the Psalmist had this in mind when he sang forth: וַתְּחַסְּרֵהוּ מְעַט מֵאֱלֹקִים (*Psalms* 8:6). You made Man small, but You invested him with a bit of G-dliness וְכָבוֹד וְהָדָר תְּעַטְּרֵהוּ (ibid.). Thereby did You crown him with glory and honor.

But Man defaces this glory, degrades this honor by attempting to deny the bit of G-d with which he has been invested. However, he becomes thereby pathetic, torn asunder by the never-ceasing drives of the eternal within him which yearns for completeness. Therein lies the tragedy of Modern Man. *Neshamah* seeks completion and fulfillment and Man feeds these burning desires with evermore *guf.* Modern Man is disillusioned. With all his success, with all his achievements, even with the conquest of outer space and the drive to dominate the moon and the planets, he lacks peace and knows not why. We live in a world where it has become commonplace to speak of the balance of terror as the determinant in world peace. Is this peace, or turmoil of the worst sort? One is prompted to recall the words of the medieval poet who wrote: גוּף וּנְשָׁמָה אִם תְּרִיבֵם דּוֹחוּ בַּל יוּכְלוּ קוּם, where there is discord between *neshamah* and *guf,* rather than harmony, neither can survive.

In this world of fear, which has become a "house of trepidation," there stands the Torah Jew, who sings forth with the Psalmist: זְמִרוֹת הָיוּ לִי חֻקֶּיךָ בְּבֵית מְגוּרָי. *Your statutes are songs of elation to me in my house of fear.*

Are the *four ells of the halachah* a small, cloistered enclave in the vast expanse of the universe, or are they the very dynamic which gives life to the cosmos? I leave this with you to ponder.

The Yeshivah Intersession

With the approach of the customary summer vacation period, we must recognize that the departure from the *bais midrash* brings with it a significant weakening in the spiritual endeavors of the *ben yeshivah*. It is proper, therefore, for us to investigate and understand the nature of study in the yeshivah — and what is the definition of *ben yeshivah*.

(1) In *Kesubos* 42b, we find the story of Akiva who began as a shepherd of Calba Savua and rose to become "the" Rabbi Akiva, the foundation of Torah *sheba'al peh*. Calba Savua's daughter perceived great potential in the shepherd — he was modest, blessed with fine character, and wholesome behavior — if so he was capable of accepting the blessing of Torah. It was she who sent him to the yeshivah to study Torah. When Calba Savua heard that his daughter married a common shepherd, he banned her from any enjoyment of his wealth. Twenty-four years later, when Rabbi Akiva returned home with 24,000 pairs of students — for the primary means of attaining Torah greatness is by studying with a partner — Calba Savua, not

---

[The Yeshivah student may look forward to the vacation weeks as a time to shed his responsibilities. In an article addressed specifically to such young people, the Rosh Yeshivah offers a Torah perspective on "free" time. From Zeirei Agudath Israel's *Daf Chizuk*, Tammuz 5740/1980. — Ed.]

knowing that the great Sage was his son-in-law, approached him seeking a nullification of his vow.

"Had you known that your daughter's husband would be a *talmid chacham*, would you have banned her?" asked Rabbi Akiva.

"Even if he were to know only one chapter or one law, I would not have done it!" (Truly astounding — Calba Savua saw in his shepherd not even the potential to know a simple law!)

Rabbi Akiva answered, "I am he, your vow is nullified!"

Tosafos (63a, ד"ה אדעתא) asks that only an *existing* condition can be used to nullify a vow on the basis of error, and at the time of Calba Savua's ban, the shepherd truly *was* a total ignoramus. *Tosafos* replies that the matter of Rabbi Akiva's knowledge was, indeed, an existing condition — *whenever someone attends a yeshivah, it may be assumed that he will become a scholar.*

Tosafos has shown us the essence of the yeshivah: it is the greenhouse that produces and develops a great man, the place where the humblest, most poorly regarded commoner becomes a Rabbi Akiva.

(2) But let us not deceive ourselves: greatness is not inevitable. The yeshivah makes great only one who *aspires* to greatness and is prepared to labor unremittingly to attain that goal. *Avos d'R' Nassan* (ch. 6) teaches us how R' Akiva began. At the age of forty he knew *nothing*. Once it was pointed out to him that dripping water had worn a groove in solid rock. He responded, "If soft water can wear away hard rock, surely the iron-hard words of Torah can wear their way into my flesh-and-blood heart." Surely this incident took place when he was on his way for the first time to the yeshivah. *Hakadosh Boruch Hu* presented him with this opportunity to galvanize his confidence and desire. Others, too, had seen the rock and the dripping water — but it took a R' Akiva to recognize that it held a lesson for *him*, and to act on it. How many years does it take for water to wear a hole in rock? How many years does it take to notice its effect? So it is with the effect of Torah study. One

who is not ready for years of effort will not only fail to be great — he will not even be a minor scholar.

We learn an important principle from R' Akiva's words: The Torah is like iron. It is unyielding, unchanging, uncompromising. Only when it is perceived and accepted by man as possessing the strength of iron can it pierce the human heart — the heart which, for all its physical frailty, is the seat of powerful lust and desire, the home of the *yetzer hara* which can overpower man's reason and lead him to deny even his Maker. R' Akiva understood this even as a shepherd — how many *bnei Torah* understand it in our time?

(3) The Sages teach us in *Midrash Eichah* that the Torah is greater in length and breadth than the length and breadth of the land. But this comparison seems incomprehensible — how does one *measure* Torah, surely not in yards and acres? We can say that Torah is more precious than gems, for then we speak of man's desire; truly rational man works hard for gems because he knows their value; he should work even harder to attain Torah knowledge because, in the scale of rational value, it is more precious than an accumulation of wealth. But the measurement of land? What yardstick does one use to measure Torah?

Certainly the *Midrash* refers not to the physical earth, but to the spiritual source of earth, the spiritual roots from which our tangible, material earth developed. Even that lofty spiritual manifestation — by whatever standard it is measured — is inferior to the Torah, according to whose blueprint *Hashem* created the immense panorama of Creation, in which is the very soul of earthly existence.

(4) To properly assess the worth of Torah — this is the primary goal of the *ben yeshivah's* labor. To whatever extent he makes part of his essence the conviction that the Torah is the universe's life-force and that only through it does he cleave to *Hashem*, to that extent he will develop as a *ben Torah*.

But it may well be that as he advances along the path of Torah knowledge, he may become so impressed with its intellectual brilliance that he will forget that its greatness is only because it is *Hashem's* Torah. This waywardness can cast him down totally, but it will be so hidden in the recesses of his soul that only *Hashem* will know. This principle is the basis of the profound words of Rabbeinu Yonah cited by Ran to explain the Sages' teaching that the Second Temple was destroyed because Israel forsook the Torah — and this abandonment of the Torah, the *Gemara* says, was expressed by a failure to make a blessing before commencing their study. *Ran* explains that they surely *did* recite the text of the blessings — otherwise their sin would have been obvious to all. Rather, their blessing failed to contain a recognition of Torah's greatness. For the obligation to make such a blessing is derived from the verse, *when I call out the Name of Hashem, (you are to) ascribe greatness to our G-d.* As *Ramban* teaches, the entire Torah consists of *Hashem's* Names. This understood, Torah study consists of constant reiteration of His Names — when Names of G-d are uttered, it follows naturally that one *must* bless Him. This is as natural as a reflex action, as the blinking of an eye when staring at the sun — the very phenomenon of Torah study — if its greatness is properly grasped, brings forth blessings of His Name. Reb Chaim Brisker and the *Minchas Chinuch* both explain, in this manner, that the blessing for Torah study is unlike the blessing over performance of a *mitzvah,* for it is not a pronouncement over an extraneous act. Not to perceive this is not to perceive Torah's nature — and it is to degrade Torah itself. For this was the Second *Beis Hamikdash* destroyed.

Similarly, *Maharal* explains why the children of *talmidei chachamim* often fail to become *talmidei chachamim* themselves. Having been exposed to the brilliance of Torah wisdom, they often take it for granted and fail to realize that its ultimate greatness is not in its intellectual content but in its spiritual grandeur.

(5) Therefore, a *ben yeshivah* must recognize what is his unique obligation. R' Yochanan says (*Shabbos* 114b with reference to *Mikvaos* 9:6) that *talmidei chachamim* are called בַּנָּאִים, *builders,* because they engage themselves in upbuilding

the world — for the holy Torah is the life-giving force of the universe. R' Chaim of Volozhin explains in *Nefesh HaChaim* that if the world is ever without Torah for even a moment, the universe would cease to exist, having been deprived of its source of life — therefore a *talmid chacham* with a spot on his garment is worthy of the death penalty, for just as *Hashem* created the world to be perfect in every detail, so must His partner in creation, the *talmid chacham*, be perfect in every detail. This perfection must be recognizable even externally, on his clothing. As the *Gaon* teaches, clothing is symbolic of the *midos* of the soul — surely, therefore, one's inner purity is reflected in his outward appearance. But it is equally true that a *ben yeshivah* whose *midos* are poor but who seeks to project a perfect outward appearance is indulging in flamboyant arrogance. Often there is but a hair breadth between truth and falsehood.

Based upon this, we can understand why R' Yochanan chose to use the word *builders*, when he discussed the special laws relating to filth on a *talmid chacham's* clothing.

6. Based on all the above — how great is the responsibility upon a *ben yeshivah* not to leave the bounds of the yeshivah even during his vacation, when he is physically out of its walls. *Maseches Kesubcs* tells us that R' Akiva returned home after twelve uninterrupted years of study. When he approached his hut, he overheard someone trying to convince his destitute wife to demand a divorce from the husband who had deserted her in favor of the *bais midrash*.

She replied, "If only he would listen to me, he would stay away to study Torah for *another* twelve years!"

Hearing her, R' Akiva turned around and returned to the yeshivah for another twelve years.

I once heard from my revered Rebbi, the Telshe Rav, הי"ד, that R' Akiva's behavior seems astounding beyond comprehension. Where was R' Akiva's consideration? In her words he recognized his wife's awesome nobility — and he was already outside her door! Couldn't he at least go in, greet her, bless her, and *then* return to the yeshivah?

But no. R' Akiva taught us a major lesson. Twenty-four is not simply two times twelve. Had he engaged in even a brief interlude of domesticity, he would have interrupted his learning. No one can measure the added greatness of learning without interruption! To a *ben yeshivah*, unwisely used vacation time can tear the fabric of his learning so that he is left with tatters of Torah time.

We must remember that every generation in whose time the *Bais Hamikdash* was not built, is regarded as if it had been destroyed in its time — because people possess freedom of choice, and they could have been worthy of the new *Bais Hamikdash*, had they so chosen *(Ramchal)*. The *ben yeshivah* is the one who has the power to become the builder of the universe, every drop accumulates in wearing away the resistance of the unwilling heart, in engraving on the heart the characteristics of the *talmid chacham*, the great man. As he ascends he raises up the world with him — to its final goal, the complete *geulah* בִּמְהֵרָה בְיָמֵינוּ אָמֵן.

In the Light of Truth

The *Yamim Noraim*, Days of Awe, is the season in Jewish life that is, by its very nature, designated for personal elevation. The preparation-days of Elul, the thoughts of repentance and soul-searching of the repentance-days demand a tenderness in the human heart, so that hearts of stone can change to hearts of flesh.

During these day, therefore, it is important to understand the definition of a Jewish heart. King David says, לְךָ אָמַר לִבִּי בַּקְשׁוּ פָנָי, *My heart says to You, O Master of the Universe, seek to know my face (Psalms 27:8).* At first glance, the verse seems to say that the *heart* is speaking, not G-d. If so, the heart should say, בַּקְשׁוּ פָנָיו, *to know His* [i.e., G-d's] *face,* meaning that the heart is appealing to us to find ways to better to know G-d. The Jewish heart is but an instrument upon which a G-dly melody is played, which calls and summons Man to an awareness of G-d. Only this is a Jewish heart. How aptly our Sages expound upon the verse אֲנִי יְשֵׁנָה וְלִבִּי עֵר, *I am asleep, but my heart is awake (Shir Hashirim 5:2):* 'My heart, this is the Holy One, Blessed is He.' The 'heart' of the Jewish people is G-d.

[As the Jew approaches the Days of Awe, the Rosh Yeshivah provides an overview on the potential and challenges of this sacred and awe-inspiring season. From the *Yamim Noraim Almanac of Dos Yiddishe Vort.* — Ed.]

Man's very essence is directed solely to the goal of recognizing the Creator, and consequently, not only his soul is bound together with the Master of the Universe, but even his body and his entire existence are rooted in the great purpose for which he is intended. The human heart — source of human will and passion — לֵב חוֹמֵד, *the heart desires* — was originally created to lust after nearness to G-d. Therefore, when a Jew locates himself upon the inner central point of his desire, he senses the flow of holiness that demands of him growth and attachment to the light of G-d. When a Jew merits to understand what is truly happening in his Jewish heart, when he hears the voice of G-d — then he is inspired, he feels the urge and the lust — אֶת פָּנֶיךָ ה' אֲבַקֵּשׁ! אַל תַּסְתֵּר פָּנֶיךָ מִמֶּנִּי, *I seek Your presence, O Hashem! Do not conceal Your presence from me (Psalms 27:8-9).*

With this we begin to sense precisely what *tefillah* is — עֲבוֹדָה שֶׁבַּלֵּב, *service of the heart.* Praying for personal needs is not *tefillah; tefillah* is a prayer to enjoy the G-dly light: אוֹר פָּנָיו יִתְבָּרַךְ, *the light of His countenance, may He be Blessed.* One is not lacking personal needs, he is lacking G-d, Blessed is He. If he finds His Creator, he has found everything. Man's many requests, that express themselves in his numerous needs — physical and spiritual — are rooted in the concealment of the G-dly light, and it is this light for which Man pleads: אַל תַּסְתֵּר פָּנֶיךָ מִמֶּנִּי, *do not conceal Your presence from me.* And when the Jew engages in prayer, when he is privileged to recognize his Creator through the first three blessings of *Shemoneh Esrei*, the blessings of אָבוֹת גְּבוּרוֹת וּקְדֻשָּׁה, *Patriarchs, Might, and Holiness,* he begins to pray that G-d should remove from him everything that interferes with his recognition of G-dliness.

He wants a clear understanding, because he cannot gain the light amid confusion. He wants to be cleansed of the sins that impede understanding. He wants health and prosperity only so that he not be deterred from this recognition. He wants to be freed from the huge impediment of exile, which is the very essence of concealment of G-d's countenance and of much more. An appreciation of the G-dly light gives Man a sense of what interferes with his recognition of it. His prayers for personal needs are directed not at the fulfillment of desires related to his animal nature, but to fulfill the higher need, the inner drive to unite with his Creator. That is why the root of *tefillah* is not the enumeration of needs, but only the call to the Creator: שְׁמַע ה' קוֹלִי אֶקְרָא, *Hear, Hashem, my voice when I call* (ibid. 27:7).

When a person succeeds in deciphering his heart's primary desire; when he senses within himself the deep desire that encompasses his entire *weltanschauung*, then he perceives the entire human tragedy — כִּי אָבִי וְאִמִּי עֲזָבוּנִי, *for my father and my mother have forsaken me* — forlorn and lonely is he in the enormous universe; וַה' יַאַסְפֵנִי, *but Hashem will gather me in.* Only the light of faith can uplift and strengthen a person. (See *Rashi to Psalms 27:7*, whose marvelous comment is taken from *Midrash Rabbah, Tazria*).

Man is terribly isolated; he finds loyal support only in G-d: רֵעֲךָ — זֶה הקב"ה, *Your friend — this is the Holy One, Blessed is He.* In this moment of the profound experience of faith, the person feels a great flow of Heavenly good, which is the only foundation and purpose of all earthly existence.

Human recognition of the Heavenly light is the central point of the Days of Awe, the time of repentance and self-evaluation, as the Sages taught us: ה' אוֹרִי וְיִשְׁעִי — 'אוֹרִי' זֶה רֹאשׁ הַשָּׁנָה יְיִשְׁעִי' זֶה יוֹם הַכִּפּוּרִים, *Hashem is my light and my salvation; 'my light,' this is Rosh Hashanah; 'and my salvation,' this is Yom Kippur.* When a person considers his life earnestly and sees how low his defects have brought him, he is faced with the enormous problem: How does one become better; how does one become different?

One who stands in the dark sees only darkness. The person must raise himself from the dark depths to the brilliant light of G-d's countenance, and then — only then — can he consider the content of his life. And then, when he raises himself up to the light, he realizes that יְסוֹדוֹ מֵעָפָר וְסוֹפוֹ לֶעָפָר, *A man's origin is from dust and his destiny is back to dust;* he is small and insignificant. And what is the content of this lowly human, who, dwelling in its darkness, thinks that he has created greatness? מָשׁוּל כְּחֶרֶס הַנִּשְׁבָּר, *he is likened to a broken shard.* But even a shard is something tangible. Man looks more deeply further and further into himself in the perspective of the light of G-d's countenance, and he realizes that he is but עָנָן כָּלָה וְרוּחַ נוֹשָׁבֶת, *a dissipating cloud, a blowing wind.* More and more he understands that he is חֲלוֹם יָעוּף, *a fleeting dream.* When man examines his existence in the light of his recognition of G-d, his existence becomes obvious as a *non*-existence.

We stand before a remarkable phenomenon. Man's lowliness and loftiness, his downfall and rise are inextricably bound up with one another. "O human child, do you wish to recognize your smallness — then raise yourself, raise yourself to the zenith of greatness. O human child, do you wish to realize that you dwell in darkness, then climb up to the pure heavens of the light of G-d's countenance!'

A Jew's entire service on this world is rooted in this. Two commandments envelop all of a Jew's identity as part of eternity: the commandments of אַהֲבַת ה' וְיִרְאַת ה', *love of Hashem and fear of Hashem.* As the *Rambam* puts it, 'What is the path toward love of *Hashen* and fear of *Hashem?* When someone meditates upon G-d's marvelous deeds and creatures, and perceives from them His wisdom, which is unbounded and immeasurable, he immediately becomes a lover of G-d. He praises Him and exalts Him, and has an insatiable desire to know the Master of the Universe. As King David said: *My soul thirsts for G-d (Psalms* 42:3). And when he meditates upon this very thing, he draws back immediately in fright, and he realizes that he is a lowly, dark creature, who stands with reduced and insignificant understanding before Him of Perfect Knowledge, as King David said (*Psalms* 8:4,5) *'When I see Your heavens ... what is frail man that You should remember him?' (Rambam, Hil. Yesodei HaTorah).*

Love of G-d is human exaltation and terrible thirst for God's closeness. To stand in His light is the recognition of the infinity of His G-dliness. And fear of G-d is the recognition of the very same light by realizing that the lowliness and fallenness of people is the source of all human suffering and tragedy. The human path is from love to fear, and not vice-versa (see also Ramban, Deuteronomy 11:11).

From all this, one begins to feel the obviousness of רֵאשִׁית חָכְמָה יִרְאַת ה', *the beginning of wisdom is fear of HASHEM* (Psalms 111:10). Fear is the direct result of love; it is rooted in the recognition of G-dly wisdom. And who perceives wisdom? Only a wise man, as King David said: מַה גָּדְלוּ מַעֲשֶׂיךָ ה', מְאֹד עָמְקוּ מַחְשְׁבֹתֶיךָ, אִישׁ בַּעַר לֹא יֵדָע, *How great are Your deeds, HASHEM; exceedingly profound are Your thoughts. A boor cannot know* (Psalms 92:6-7). Upon the verse הֵן יִרְאַת ה' הִיא חָכְמָה, *Behold, fear of G-d — this is wisdom* (Job 28:28), our Sages say that the word הֵן is to be understood as *one* or *identical*; i.e., wisdom is identical with fear of G-d only if it *leads* to such fear. All aspects of wisdom in this world are sparks from the great Source of Perfect Wisdom, Blessed is He. If someone attaches himself to the spark without recognizing the Source, his wisdom is empty; without soul or content. He who sees only the sparks sees only many isolated aspects of wisdom, but true wisdom that has its origin in fear of G-d is unified, for it represents the recognition of G-d's wisdom, the source of all wisdom.

The light to which Man is privileged on *Rosh Hashanah* is the light of wisdom, the light of love, of great thirst and yearning for *Hashem*, Blessed is He. All year long this is an enormously difficult task, but *Hashem* did Man the kindness of granting him the period of the Days of Awe, with its flow of heavenly inspiration. He lowers Himself to humanity so that He can uplift humanity, to cleanse and purify it. It is for Man to utilize the potential granted him, through strenuous effort during this period, to illuminate his entire inner self and lift it out of downfall and darkness. And in direct proportion to how much Man merits the illumination of love of *Hashem*, he simultaneously merits the trembling of fear, the deep glimpse into man's puniness. And in direct proportion to how profoundly he perceives this puniness, he realizes that everything that originates in this smallness is insignificant, without content, but an empty dream.

From such a clear recognition, Man arrives at deep regret over his past, and he lifts himself to great undertakings for his future; an undertaking that is unclouded by doubt, clear and direct. Every recognition that emanates from the light of G-dly truth is clear and without perplexity. At the moment of such an undertaking, Man is in a position of such exaltation that G-d — Who alone sees all that is hidden — attests that such a person will not regress to his human foolishness. And if he does so regress, it is only because he has again drawn back from the light of G-dly truth to which he had raised himself, and has returned to the shadow of Divine concealment.

זֶה יוֹם הַכִּפּוּרִים — 'וְיִשְׁעִי, 'And my salvation' — this is Yom Kippur. When the Jew reaches the ultimate recognition of the illumination offered by G-d's truth — at the climax of the Ten Days that He has designated just for this possibility — and when he has thereby completely perceived and sensed Man's insignificance, and without hesitation set out his path toward the future — at that very moment has Man been privileged to receive G-d's salvation. He has been redeemed from his degradation, from the darkness of human lowliness. Then he has already been vindicated in judgment, and is ready to live through the forthcoming festival of soulful joy — זְמַן שִׂמְחָתֵנוּ, the season of our joy!

Talmudic Jurisprudence

We will attempt, within the limited scope of one article, to present a fragmentary concept of that great body of law known as Talmudic Jurisprudence, and in so doing, it will be our purpose to determine what Talmudic Law can contribute towards the solution of the problems of our troubled world.

The purpose of the Law, as civilized society understands it, is to bring order into the lives and affairs of men, to guarantee — to use a Mishnaic phrase — that "men shall not swallow themselves alive" (*Avos* 3:2, cf. *Psalms* 124:3). Where order exists in society humankind can develop to the fullest extent its capacities for progress under freedom and liberty. A society governed by the Law is therefore given a guarantee against anarchy, against chaos and disintegration.

Though this be the purpose of the Law, yet the Law itself can become cold and sometimes even cruel if it is designed only to meet the requisites of an ordered society. Indeed, there is a law even among barbarians. The cruelty and tyranny of the dictator is also framed in the order of law. One is reminded of

[In a precedent-setting and warmly received initiative, Western Reserve University invited the Rosh Yeshivah to lecture on Talmudic Jurisprudence and how it relates to society. From *Law In a Troubled World*, published by The Press of Western Reserve University, Cleveland, Ohio. — Ed.]

the words of the Psalmist who, in speaking of the tyrant, describes him as being one "who frames violence by statute" (Psalms 94:20).

The development of civilized law knows, therefore, also of the development of equity in the law. Equity has served, we might say, as a guardian over the law, seeking to keep it in line with ethical norms.

It has *not* been the purpose of the law, however, even when joined with equity, to develop the moral and ethical standards of society and of the individual. This has been the domain of philosophy and of religion. These values nurtured by philosophy, religion and other kindred branches of ethical and moral teaching became the norms within which the law developed and fructified.

Talmudic jurisprudence is unique in that the very purpose of the law, itself, is the development of Man's moral and ethical personality. The ambit of Talmudic Law is a very wide one, indeed, the widest one can imagine, for its scope embraces every facet of human living. It is by no means limited to that body of legal matter encompassed by the term "law" as we know it in modern society; namely, that which concerns itself only with t'iose affairs of man vis-a-vis his fellow man. Since its purpose is order in society, it deals with man as part of society, its ambit being the world of human relations. Man, the individual, per se, is not the object of the law. Certainly the conscience of the individual is outside the scope of the law.

Not so with Talmudic jurisprudence. The very same law which deals with torts, bailments, contracts, and criminal offenses deals also with Man's duties of prayer, of ritual and ceremonial, yea, even with problems of faith in the Divine Creator. Just as the Rabbinic Court was bid to enforce a contract, so was it bid to enforce the observance of the building of the *succah* on the Feast of Tabernacles. Idolatry in Talmudic law is of the same degree as the criminal offense of murder, subject to the death penalty.

The gamut of the *Beis-Din Hagadol*, the High Court, the supreme authority of the law, included such diverse matters as the case of the false prophet, the High Priest who had committed a capital offense, the decision to declare war, extending the boundaries of Jerusalem and of the Temple courts, appointing district courts and decisions involving interpretation of the law. The law embraced all of life, public as well as private, individual as well as social in character.

The ultimate authority for Talmudic law is the Torah, the Five Books of Moses, containing the Commandments of the Lord revealed at Sinai, and thereafter, through Moses. Since the ultimate authority of the law is the Commandment of God, there is no room left for man outside the framework of the law. All is open before Him "who tests the hearts of men."

The law, therefore, in the Talmudic sense, is the revelation of the Divine Commandment, of the demands made upon man to raise himself above the level of the beast. It is the law which says to man: "See, I set before thee life and good and death and evil, and thou shalt choose life" *(Deuteronomy 30:15-19)*. It is the law which posits the freedom of Man to choose the path to nobility and human dignity, the freedom of the individual to determine and direct his destiny, that freedom which is the primary source and the ultimate goal of the sovereignty of the people revolting against the yokes of all forms of tyranny. Maimonides terms this freedom "the pillar of the Law and the Commandment" *(Hil. Teshuvah 5:3)*. But yet the law, in stating this great human principle, bids and commands Man as to the direction of his choice. Within this commandment, "Thou shalt choose life," therein is contained the entire body of the law, embracing all which is life.

The law is so many times identified, in the language of the Torah, with righteousness — "righteous statutes and judgments" *(Deuteronomy 4:8)* — for its purpose is to make of Man a righteous being, who has chosen freely to be governed by moral and ethical values. The basic premise of the law is the never-ceasing consciousness that one stands always in the presence of his Creator. In order to insure this goal the law sees the necessity for a complete system regulating the conduct of Man, not merely in dealing with his fellow-man, but also in dealing with himself. For he who attempts to achieve moral and ethical perfection and integrity in himself will, of necessity, deal in kind with his fellow-man. Society is molded of the individuals who build it. An ordered and disciplined personality in the individual guarantees a well-balanced and harmonious society.

How striking are the words of the Torah when commanding the judge to be completely impartial and objective, not to be influenced by the fear of men. Why? "For justice is of G-d" (Deuteronomy 4:8). The court is but the instrument of the will and of the commandment of Him who created the judge, the plaintiff, and the defendant. How ennobling for all concerned to feel that they stand in the presence of G-d when seeking justice in the court of law!

The student of the Talmud is acquainted with the phrases "Rachmana amar, Rachmana kasav [רַחְמָנָא אֲמַר, רַחְמָנָא כָּתַב], the Merciful One has said, the Merciful One has written" (Bava Kamma 5b). The law is an expression of Divine mercy evidenced in the desire, apparent in the Commandment, to raise and elevate Man to the level of that law designed for Man. And often our opinion would dictate a more stringent liability, but Rachmina chas alei, the Merciful One has eased the penalty" (Bava Kamma 15a). Laws in civil liabilities become lessons in Divine mercy. Is this not a unique approach to law?

That great pillar of Talmudic jurisprudence, Maimonides, created the greatest comprehensive codification of Talmudic law. It seems apparent that he considered his Code as an elaborate commentary upon the six hundred and thirteen commandments of the Torah. He first created his Sefer Hamitzvos, the Book of Commandments, containing the cardinal principles in determining the essence of a commandment of the Torah, and thereupon enumerating the six hundred and thirteen commandments based upon these principles. He then proceeded to elaborate upon this work by codifying the entire body of Talmudic law. Every division in his Code, therefore, is introduced with an enumeration of the mitzvos, the commandments, dealt with in the respective division of the Code. This is indicative of the Talmudic approach to the law. The law is the commandment of G-d revealed in the Torah, developed and expostulated down through the ages. A discussion of the law in the Talmudic academies of learning is an attempt to understand the will of G-d in directing the conduct and affairs of Man.

Lest we leave the impression that Talmudic law is primarily theologic in nature it might be of value to make mention of some points of law which engage the attention of the student of the Talmud.

We are engaged, presently, at the Telshe Yeshivah in the study of the tractate Bava Kamma in the Mishnaic Order of Nezikin — Injuries. This tractate deals primarily with torts resulting from injury. The first portion of the tractate is concerned with damages resulting from injury caused by personal property. The Torah speaks of the "goring ox" for which the owner is liable as "a Man's ox" (Exodus 21:35-36), the ox belonging to a person. It also mentions the fact that "its owner hath not kept it in." The liability for damages is conditioned by two requisites; that the ox be the property of a person and that the owner shall not have exercised prudent care over the ox. Hence the principle enunciated in the first mishnah of Bava Kamma is that of "your property and subject to your care." The question arises: What is the primary cause of liability? Is it "ownership" — the fact that the injury was caused by your personal property, in which case the clause "subject to your care" is not the cause of liability but rather a ground for defense to free you from liability if you had exercised proper care; or is the clause "subject to your care" the cause of liability, your negligence in not exercising prudent care, in which case the clause "your property" is merely the reason for your obligation to perform proper care? In brief, does liability presuppose a fault or is the lack of fault merely ground for defense? This is a basic problem in the fundamental principle of the law with many practical effects resulting therefrom. We shall mention a few.

Suppose the ox belonged to a minor. A minor cannot be held

responsible for personal negligence. If liability results from the fault of the owner, a minor is free of fault. If liability results from ownership the minor would also be liable, for the fact of his being a minor does not create grounds for defense.

Another practical effect. Let us suppose there is a doubt as to whether the owner had exercised proper care. If ownership is the cause for liability, a doubtful defense cannot free the owner of his liability. If, however, negligence is the cause of liability, proof would have to be brought for negligence and the burden of such proof would rest upon the person who suffered the damages.

Yet another practical effect. Let us suppose the owner gave the ox to an agent for keeping and the agent had not exercised proper care. If negligence is the cause for liability then the agent should be liable, since agency also places the responsibility of proper care upon the agent and we have here the fault of negligence caused by agency even though it not be "ownership." If, however, "ownership" is the cause for liability, an agent should not be liable. However, it is possible that agency constitutes a new category of liability, acting in place of the owner and therefore liable by the principle of "ownership."

The basic problem involved has not yet, to my knowledge, been definitely resolved. (The student will find enlightenment on the subject in the following works: *Even Haezel, Nizkei Mamon* I,1; *Shiurei Halachah* — R' Joseph L. Bloch, 75-76; *Mehkarim B'Talmud* — R' J.J. Weinberg, 180-191.)

Such problems in civil law also represent human striving to dignity and nobility, a desire to attune human conduct to the will of G-d. This is the basis of the principle posited by the great medieval Talmudic jurist, R' Shlomo Ibn Aderes, who states that questions involving doubts of interpretation of the basic law in injuries are governed by the principle used in resolving doubts in ritual law rather than the principle applied in resolving doubts relating to money values (Novellae *Rashba Bava Kamma* 3b).

The effort expended in trying to solve the problem is, from

the viewpoint of Talmudic law, an attempt to discern the intent of the Divine Commandment pertaining to the goring ox, so that men may govern themselves in accordance with that Divine will and authority.

We find a most interesting and unique feature in Talmudic law. We read in the Talmud: Rabba Bar Bar-Chana had a barrel of wine broken through the negligence of laborers hired to transport the wine. Rabba, thereupon, seized the laborers' cloaks as a lien for damages, something permissible by law. The laborers complained to the great master, Rav, who directed Rabba to return the cloaks. Rabba asked Rav: "Is this then the law?" And Rav answered: "Yes, for it is written, 'That thou shall walk in the path of the virtuous' (Psalms 2:20)." Rabba returned the cloaks. The laborers then said to Rav: "We are poor, we have labored all day and we are hungry, but we have not the means to purchase food." Rav, thereupon, said to Rabba: "Pay them their hire." Rabba asked: "Is this the law?" And Rav answered: "Yes, for it is written, 'And the paths of the righteous shalt thou keep' " (Bava Metzia 83a)

The ruling of the court in this case was not prompted by the recognition of the equity and justice in the claim of the plaintiffs for, indeed, they had no claim at all. Rather was it prompted by the realization that the ultimate purpose of the law is to develop a disciplined personality, fully imbued with personal morals and ethics. No doubt, the ruling was delivered by Rav because the defendant was Rabba Bar Bar-Chana, an individual who had proved himself worthy of higher moral demands and standards. The ruling of the court took into consideration the ethical norms of the individuals involved. This is in accordance with the general principle known as "lifnim mishuras hadin" — going beyond the line of the law, which, in this particular case, was equated by Rav with "din" — the line of the law itself.

It is quite apparent that this is not a question of an equity which seeks to have the law meet ethical norms, but rather reveals a desire on the part of the law to inject its inner spirit and purpose into the ruling of the court. It is a part of that body of law which describes a lawsuit in terms of "unto the L-rd shall their dispute come" *(Exodus* 22:8; cf. *Deuteronomy* 19:17, *Rashi* et al.).

All which we have attempted to say is so beautifully presented in the poetic language of the Midrash. Solomon, in his Song of Songs, speaks of the people of Israel as being like unto a "heap of wheat set about with a hedge of roses" *(Song of Songs* 7:3; see *Midrash Rabbah* ad loc.). The Rabbis of the Midrash comment thereon: The hedge of roses, these are the words of the Torah, which are as delicate as the rose. Said Rabbi Levi:

> *"A tempting dish is brought before a person. He prepares to partake of it with great relish. He is told that tallow [i.e., forbidden animal fat] has fallen into the food and he refrains even from tasting it. Who has caused this restraint? What serpent has bitten him? What scorpion has stung him to keep him from drawing near to the food to taste of it? Only the words of the Torah, delicate as the rose, for it is written: 'You shall not eat the fat' (Leviticus 3:17)."*

And yet another illustration (see *Rashi, Song of Songs* ad loc.). A person was walking along a country road. He passed a fruit orchard and the fragrance of the fully ripened, first fruits of the season attracted him. He stretched forth his hand to pick a fruit from the tree. He was reminded: These fruits have an owner. He drew back his hand in restraint. What has caused this restraint? What stands between him and the fruit? Only the words of the Torah, delicate as the rose, for it is written: "Thou shalt not rob" *(Leviticus* 19:13).

For the aesthete who has developed an appreciation for the beauty and delicacy of the rose, a hedge of roses is stronger than a wall of iron. He needs but the rose itself to serve as a barrier against trespass. For one reared and nurtured in the law, transgression is trespass.

Man, created in the image of G-d, is inherently good and noble, striving to fulfill the Divine will which inheres within him *(Maimonides, Hil. Gerushin* 2:20). That world of passion, lust and temptation which makes goodness and nobility so difficult to realize, must find its remedy in the law. Man is called upon to develop within himself, through the law, an aesthetic appreciation of moral and ethical values — an ever-present G-d consciousness. The word of the law is the gentle reminder to refrain from trespass in the human soul, handiwork of Almighty G-d.

But certainly a code of law designed to be studied only by lawyers cannot achieve the purpose of which we speak. The law cannot lead men to the lofty heights of morals and ethics, nor can it serve as a guide for the disciplined conduct of the individual, if it remains beyond the reach of the individual. The loftiest principle, therefore, of Talmudic law is the exhortation to study the law, an exhortation directed towards every individual, not only to these who seek their profession in the law.

It is of interest, in this connection, to quote from Josephus in *Against Apion* (Book II, 18; Tr. Whiston).

> *Moses did not suffer the guilt of ignorance to go on without punishment, but demonstrated the law to be the best and most necessary instruction of all others, permitting the people to leave off their other employments and to assemble together for the hearing of the law and learning it exactly. And this not once or twice, or oftener, but every week, which thing all the other legislators seem to have neglected. And indeed, the greatest part of Mankind are so far from living according to their own laws, that they hardly know them; but when they have sinned they learn from others that they have transgressed the law. Those also who are in the highest and principal posts of the government confess they are not acquainted with those laws and are obliged to take such persons for their assessors in public administrations as profess to have skill in those laws. But for our people, if anybody do but ask anyone of them about our laws, he will more readily tell them all than he will his own name. And this in consequence of our having learned them immediately, as*

soon as ever we became sensible of anything, and of having them as it were engraven on our souls.

So wrote an historian recording Jewish life at about the beginning of the common era.

Maimonides, in his Code, has a division devoted to the laws of Torah study. Therein he postulates *(Talmud Torah I,8)*: Every male person in Israel is obligated to study Torah, be he poor or rich, healthy or subject to suffering, young or so old that his strength is ebbing, even if he be burdened with wife and children, he is obligated to set aside a specific time by day and by night to study Torah, for it is written: "Thou shalt study it by day and by night."

This Commandment, this law to study the law, is the quintessential of Talmudic jurisprudence. We quote from Talmudic literature *(Avos d' R' Nassan 6:2).*

What were the beginnings of R' Akiva? It is said: When he was forty years of age he had not yet studied Talmud. Once he stood by the mouth of a well. There he noticed a well-stone. "Who has hollowed out the stone?" he asked. He was told it was the water which fell upon it every day continually. He wondered at this. It was said to him: "Akiva, has thou not read: 'The waters wear away the stones?' (Job 14:19)." Thereupon R' Akiva drew the implication for himself. "If what is soft wears down the hard, all the more shall the words of the Torah, which are as hard as iron (i.e., in their unbending and unchanging demands upon man), hollow out my heart which is but flesh and blood!" With this he dedicated himself to the study of Torah.

The law, through continuous, endless study, can make of Man's heart a receptacle for the living waters of moral and ethical perfection. For, as we quote from Rambam:

Every human being has the characteristic that when he is attracted to the ways of wisdom and righteousness, he yearns for them and pursues them (Hil. Teshuvah 6:5).

Talmudic law is common law in the sense that its knowledge is common for all men and not the domain of the professional student of the law. The law is therefore truly a Torah — a system of instruction to the people embracing all the problems of life, seeking to make the people worthy of the great heritage of humanity — Man created in the image of G-d (cf. *Mishnah Avos* 3:8).

I think we have made some points, though of necessity quite superficial, which, if digested and taken to heart, will be found to have great bearing upon the problems besetting us in these troubled times. Freedom and liberty under law rather than violence under tyranny, this is the great problem of our day. The further the advance of science in developing nuclear energy and in conquering outer space, the greater is the poignancy of this problem. The law, Divine in essence, brought to all the people to lead and guide them to the heights of human nobility and dignity — therein lies our strength and security as free men.

Ahavas Chessed

Ages ago there lived in Canaan, Avraham, forefather of the *Bnei Yisroel* — Children of Israel. His life was spent in proclaiming G-d's sovereignty over the lives of men. His efforts, sincere and pure, were appreciated by his contemporaries, even those who could not see eye to eye with him. And they called him *Nesi Elokim* — Prince of G-d.

Avraham spread his great message to mankind through a method fine and noble. He felt that a person does not by any means live for his own selfish interests alone. Every human being is part of the great family of Mankind; and if one is really to enjoy life, he must share with others that which has been granted to him.

The needy wayfarer — fatigued, hungry and thirsty — must be brought into the home. He must be given the opportunity to rest before traveling further. Food and drink must be served to him. After refreshing himself, he is ready to go on — provided also with food for the journey. Avraham felt, however, that he had more than this to share with the needy. G-d had also granted him the spiritual bounty of knowing and realizing that

[A Jewish school should nourish the heart as well as the mind. The Rosh Yeshivah presents the Torah view of this essential aspect of the *chinuch* process. From *The Jewish Parent*, Dec. 1950-Jan. 1951. Ed.]

it was the Almighty Himself who provided him with all his needs. Avraham was blessed with *"Emunah"* — deep faith — which permeated his entire being. These great spiritual riches must also be shared with others.

It was not merely a question of sharing with others because of the needs of those others. No, it was indeed far more than that. Avraham felt that all which had been bestowed upon him, physically and spiritually, was of value to him only insofar as it was given and imparted to others. If the occasion for acts of kindness did not arise, Avraham felt a deep personal loss. His riches became atrophied within him for lack of activation. Indeed, to converse with G-d himself, without being given the opportunity of sharing with others, became a source of deep sorrow to Avraham. Small wonder, indeed, that men recognized Avraham as the Prince of G-d.

Ma'asei Avos simon le'vonim — "the acts of our forefathers are symbols unto their offspring." How noble, how deeply inspiring is an act of kindness which is rooted in the *chessed* — kindness and goodness — preached and practiced by Avraham *Avinu*. To dwell and elaborate upon the *"Parshas Hachessed"* of Avrohom *Avinu* as pictured by the Torah and interpreted by our Sages is the best technique that can possibly be employed in conveying the lesson of *chessed* to our children.

How are we to convey to our children this great lesson — one of the principal motifs in the moral and ethical beauty of Torah *Yiddishkeit?* As in all problems of *chinuch*, the first thing which we must bear in mind is the necessity that the educator himself, whether he be parent or teacher, set an example for the child in his own personal life. The inspired parent and teacher is our greatest educational asset.

The charity box, both at home and in the classroom, should not be taken by the child as a matter of course. He must be taught the meaning of his charity. Here we have an excellent opportunity to point out to the child that although his few pennies may not actually do much toward alleviating distress, yet the act itself does mean a great deal for his personal development.

The teacher should never fail to have the idea of *chessed* occupy an important place in classroom decoration. Classroom decoration should always have definite educational purposes in view.

If we have honor rolls for perfection in studies and attendance, we should have the same for perfection in character development. *Ahavas chessed* is the foundation of that portion of Torah which we term *bain adam lechavero* — between man and his fellow man. It is, therefore, of prime importance that the child be given an incentive to develop within himself this great character trait. But for this purpose it is greatly necessary that the child become acquainted with various ramifications within *ahavas chessed* which have bearing upon the child's life in school, at home, and in the outside world.

Friendship with classmates, pleasant relations with other members of the family, cooperation and team work, all so important in the progress and development of the child, are really part of the general theme of *chessed*. They should, therefore, be presented and taught to the child as such.

A very important lesson that must be taught to the child is *chessed Hashem* — the fact that we are continually enjoying the loving kindness of *Hashem Yisborach*. And from this vantage point, the child should be impressed with the importance of performing acts of kindness to others. This is what our Sages taught us long, long ago: "*Ma Hu rachum, af atah rachum* — Just as the Almighty is merciful, so must you be merciful!"

Ahavas chessed, if presented in the light of Torah, can become a *kraka dekola bei*, a veritable storehouse of all that is fine and noble in Torah *Yiddishkeit*.

Judaism in Practice

◆§ Introduction

A living, vibrating, Torah Judaism has as its prime purpose the continual, never-ceasing molding of the Jewish personality as an entity of G-d-consciousness. "I have set G-d always before me" *(Tehillim* 16:8) is the opening axiom of our *Shulchan Aruch.*

The world of Jewish thought alone cannot fulfill this purpose. The deepest and most inspiring thought, if not translated into action, into deeds, becomes atrophied and stagnant. The Rabbis said long ago, "The essence is not study, but deeds!" And the deed, the *mitzvah,* is void of content if it is not the result of previous preparation. And so again the Rabbis said, "Study is great, for it leads to deeds." Torah Judaism is therefore the depth of thought translated into the height of action — the inspired deed of *mitzvah.*

The performance of *mitzvos* in the correct manner and spirit must therefore be recognized as a basic feature in the process of Jewish education — both for young and old.

The celebration of our Jewish festivals and holidays is one of

[In a series of articles addressed to parents, the Rosh Yeshivah guides them through the year, showing how to imbue the home atmosphere with the values of the holy days. From *The Jewish Parent,* 1954-5. — Ed.]

the great sources of *mitzvah* education. Every Jewish holiday has its own specific motif — its specific place in the symphonic harmony of the Jewish soul.

Just as the musical instrument must first be tuned before it can be played on, so the Jew must attune himself to the holiday which is about to touch upon his soul-strings.

The material problems of a fatiguing day must be allowed to pass from the mind and heart if the Jew wishes to enjoy properly the benefits of the Jewish holiday. A parent prepared for the holiday is automatically an educator of his child in Jewish observance.

Shabbos

The Jew is singular in that his Torah way of thinking teaches him that time is an essential element in Creation. Though time is not something to be encompassed by the physical sense, yet it is a reality which often determines the nature of those things perceived by the senses.

All things material must in the Torah-Jew's philosophy of life be elevated into the realm of the spirit, the world of *mitzvah.* This can be accomplished by the infusion of Divine Will and Command into daily living. Time, although *unmaterial*, is not *immaterial* in the life of the Torah-Jew. And because of its very unmateriality, it must not be permitted to become a mere instrument to the material, but rather it must become sanctified through the Divinity of *mitzvah.* And so we have been given *mitzvot* whose essential feature is *kedushas hazman* — sanctity of time.

All the *Yamim Tovim* consist of *mitzvos* ordained to take certain moments of time and make them moments of eternity through union with *Hashem Yisborach*, the Almighty, in the fulfillment of His Divine Will.

There is, however, one moment which serves as the repository of this entire soul-inspiring concept of *kedushas hazman.* And that is the *Shabbos* — the Sabbath — the *yom techilah lemikro'ei kodesh*, the first of the holidays.

In relating to us the story of Creation, the Torah points to the divisions of time involved therein. The seventh day was that portion of time free from the act of Creation and designated for *berachah* and *kedushah*, blessing and sanctity. The *Shabbos* is therefore indicative of G-d's Supremacy in Creation. The *Shabbos* is that moment in time which lifts the Jew into that which preceded Creation — the moment of *me'ein olam haba* — a bit of the world to come — in *olam hazeh* — in this world. It is no wonder, therefore, that the *Shabbos* is the *os beini uvein bnei Yisrael*, the sign of covenant between G-d and Israel.

Shabbos is not merely a day of rest. If it were so, the pagan nations who considered the Jew lazy for his *Shabbos* observance — and even an intellectual like Seneca taunted the Jew for his *Shabbos* — would have been right. The *menuchah* of *Shabbos* is not *rest from work*, rather it is *rest for contemplation* of the Divine in life — the moment given to Man to perceive the *neshamah yeseirah* — the additional soul of life.

The Torah-Jew views with pity his brothers who have lost the *Shabbos* from their lives. For them, time is a mere monotone, an instrument in their world of material things and affairs. The Torah has taken portions of the *Shabbos* moment and strewn them into the life of the Jew in the various *Yamim Tovim* throughout the year, each *Yom Tov* another opportunity to sanctify time, to save it from being crushed under material things.

Here in this country, it has become customary to say, "Time is money," but the Chofetz Chaim, of sainted memory, used to say, "Money is time." The difference in concept is the difference between day and night, between light and darkness, between spiritual and material, between *Shabbos* and the *sheishes yemei hamaaseh* — the six days of Creation.

Parents should take advantage of every facet provided by the *Shabbos* for elevation and inspiration. It should not be allowed to become only a day of physical rest from the fatigue of the entire week. The *Shabbos* meals are part of *Shabbos* observance. One of our *Tannaim* once explained to a Roman official that the *Shabbos* delicacies derived their taste from the *Shabbos* spirit of the Jew. The *Shabbos zemiros* are another opportunity for inspiration. Discussion of the weekly portion of the Torah should not be overlooked. Reviewing the child's accomplishments at school during the week are a must for the *Shabbos*. All this serves to make the *Shabbos* a day of *kedushah* and *berachah*.

"Taste" the *Shabbos* and give your child a portion of *olam haba*.

Yamim Noraim

The need for self-evaluation is the motif of the *Yamim Noraim* — the Days of Awe, Rosh Hashanah and Yom Kippur. Life must be governed by periods of retrospect in which Man is able to examine himself in the light of past experiences and future hopes. Therein lies the secret of that great idea called *teshuvah* — which connotes much more than the term *penitence*, usually used as its English equivalent.

The entire month of Elul serves as a preparatory period for the *Yamim Noraim*. The daily blowing of the *Shofar* is the reminder for a change in attitude, a stronger and more powerful consciousness of the fact that we alone are not masters of our destiny. Once the Jew begins to feel this he becomes conscious of a yearning towards G-d. And with this yearning, there comes the realization of his personal unworthiness in the light of G-d's boundless Greatness — Great both in Judgment and in Mercy. When these thoughts begin to penetrate the Jew's consciousness, he begins to see himself as part of the vast and universal plan of creation, and is no longer self-centered.

And so, when *Rosh Hashanah* arrives, the Jew does not stand in supplication for personal needs. Rather the *tefillos* are an expression of the recognition of G-d's endless power as Master of the Universe, finding in Judgment the place for compassion and mercy, the source of which lies in *Zichronos* — in the collective repository of Israel's past, leading ultimately to universal recognition of the Divine Presence in Creation.

There follows the period of *Aseres Yemei Teshuvah* in which the Jew deepens and broadens the consciousness of Divinity which is beginning to permeate his being. And all this culminates in the glory of a *Yom Kippur* — when through complete abstinence from earthly matters the Jew reaches a state of Divine proximity which carries with it purification and expiation.

Now certainly the depth of Jewish consciousness which the *Yamim Noraim* contain is not something which a Jewish child can learn through study. It is too profound for a child's mind and for that matter even for many an adult. Yet, it is chiefly by study that the mind and heart can become opened to such profound influences. But this must be accompanied by the living example set by parents. If the parent begins to feel the approach of the *Yamim Noraim*, if there begins to live within the parent a fear of the impending *Yom Hadin*, then the child will unconsciously react to the motif of this specific period in the Jewish year.

The warmth and fervor of the *tefillos* on the *Yamim Noraim* are certainly a great source for Divine inspiration. But this calls for *tefillah* in its proper environment, not in that of the *chazzanic* glamorization and commercialization of the *Yamim Noraim*. It is the responsibility of the parent to choose and find the proper *shul* and the child should observe pious *tefillah*, not merely musical incantation.

It must be remembered that the *Yamim Noraim* are *Yamim Tovim*. They are not days of a backward despairing spirit. They are days of a renewed spiritual power and struggle. The specific dishes, such as the carrots and honey, which serve to symbolize the hope for acceptance of our prayers, help to enhance the *Yom Tov* spirit. It is a *Yom Tov* tempered with solemnity, but it is by no means a day of sorrow and sadness. It is the concept of *V'gilu Biradah* — Be "joyous" in "trembling."

Shabbos Shuvah should be used by the parent for good purpose. A discussion with the child — on his level — as to the aspects of the *Yamim Noraim* would be most advisable. Stories concerning the *Gedolei Yisrael* of the past and their observance of the *Yamim Noraim* are a great source of inspiration and leave an indelible impression upon the child. The feeling of personal unworthiness, which is such an integral part of the *Yamim Noraim*, is a very important factor in controlling the natural instincts of the personal ego, which many times hampers the healthy spiritual development of the child. The *Yamim Noraim* will teach him that Man is greatest on his knees.

The lesson that mistakes and misdeeds can be rectified where there is a sincere desire is also of great importance in the development of the child's personality. And this idea of *teshuvah* can be painted for the child in his own colors. It will remain with him as a never-forgotten picture.

Succos

Following the *Yamim Noraim* with their profundity of thought, there comes the festival of *Succos*, so rich with the symbolism of *mitzvah* acts. The *Arba Minim* and the *succah* keep the Jew surrounded with *mitzvos* for an entire *Yom Tov*.

The motif of the *Yom Tov* is that of *simchah* — joy and elation. After the purification of the *Yamim Noraim*, the Jew bursts forth with divine elation, prepared with the spiritual nurture for the new year. Every day is another occasion for reciting the *Hallel*.

The Jew is blessed with the great guests who visit him in the *succah*, the seven *Ushpizin*, the *Avos*, Avrohom, Yitzchok, Yaakov, Yoseph *HaTzaddik*, Moshe, Aharon, and David. The invitation extended to the *Ushpizin* prior to the *Yom Tov* meal tends to enhance the sanctity of the *simchah*.

A *Yom Tov* replete with so many acts of *mitzvos* should give an opportunity for the child to enjoy its benefits. If possible the child should have his own *lulav* and *esrog*. We can well imagine the sense of pride in the *mitzvah* this would give him. Have him participate in the *Simchas Beis Hashoeivah*. Let him sing and make merry, knowing that this is *mitzvah*, Divine service. Have him study Torah in the *succah*. What other opportunity is there to actually "breathe" and "inhale" *mitzvah* into the Jewish soul!

Simchas Torah

It is hard to imagine a more fitting ending to the cycle of Tishri festivals than that of *Simchas Torah*. What are the festivals, if not one of the facets of Torah expression in Jewish life?

On *Simchas Torah* all the elements of joy become united in the one source of all Jewish living, in Torah itself. But what is Torah without Jewish children, our future scholars — *Gedolei Yisroel*. And so for ages children have been the *yachsonim* of *Simchas Torah*. So much so that one of the *aliyos* has been designated for them, the *Kol Hanearim*.

In the many customs of *Simchas Torah* there is revealed the Jew's devotion and boundless love of Torah. With that love he is prepared to forge ahead for a new year of trial and achievement.

Chanukah

Chanukah has become a festival in Jewish life although it lacks, in its origin, all the elements of the *Yamim Tovim*. These eight days were originally days dedicated to *Hallel* and *Hoda'ah* — Praise and Thanksgiving for the miracle of salvation from the Greek hordes. It has but one ceremonial, the *mitzvah* of kindling the lights.

The lesson of Chanukah, however, has served to give to it the aura of a *Yom Tov*. The meaning of faith, the Almighty's guardianship of Israel, are driven home in the story of Chanukah. Israel's feeling that salvation is not man-made is conveyed in the *Hallel* and *Hoda'ah*. The *mitzvah* of kindling lights is soul-inspiring. The requirements of *parsumei nisa*— publicizing the miracle — by kindling the lights where they will be seen from the outside is a source of pride in our heritage of *emunah*.

Jewish children react with warmth and inspiration to the observance, the kindling of lights. They should be allowed the privilege of having their own lamp. The singing of *Haneros Hallalu* and *Ma'oz Tzur* should be conducted by the parents, displaying interest in these songs. Just getting it over with kills an opportunity for spiritual nurture on an elevated level in the child.

The story of Chanukah can be acquired in English and children should read and know the story. They should be well acquainted with the heroism of the *Chashmonaim*. They should be impressed with the fact that G-d's holy priests, the *Kohanim*, and their religious followers — who died for the sanctity of the *Shabbos* — had the courage to bear arms and rise in battle against the Greeks. They should become impressed with the fact that the religious Jew, the Torah Jew, is perfectly capable of coping with Israel's national and international problems.

One of the greatest necessities in Jewish education today is the creation of the realization that Torah is all-embracing. Our children must become infused with the feeling that being religious Jews does not place limitations upon them but rather opens for them the broadest vista upon life and all its problems. The story of Chanukah, if learned through its true perspective, can help greatly in this direction. This means that there must be a careful selection of the reading material on Chanukah. Many of the truths of Jewish history have been distorted and the story of Chanukah has also been subjected to the surgery of historical falsification.

The Chanukah play in school is another means for enriching the child's inspiration with the Chanukah heritage. However, it might be advisable to point out here that preparation for the Chanukah play should not be a reason for slowing up the daily program of study. This defeats the very purpose of the festivity. In our best Day Schools we cannot afford to lose any time devoted to study.

Taanis Esther

The purpose of the fast days in the annual Jewish cycle of living is "to arouse the heart to the ways of penitence, to become conscious of our faults and the faults of our forebears which were the cause of their trials and tribulations commemorated by the fast day. It is by such cognition that we will be able to better our ways" *(Rambam,* Hil. Taaniyos ch. 5).

The Fast of Esther precedes the celebration of Purim in order to make us more conscious of the *nes* — the miracle — of Purim. Just as fasting and prayer preceded the original miracle, so also do we seek to enhance the inspiration of the celebration of salvation with fasting and prayer.

The Fast has no symbolism connected with its observance. The penitential *Selichos* prayers are therefore the only source for giving meaning and content to this day. It is imperative, therefore, that the parent attend these prayer services together with the child who is already of age.

Mere recitation of the *Selichos* prayers without knowledge of their meaning will be of little value. It would be well for the parent to acquaint himself with the content of the *Selichos* and at the same time to acquaint his child with their content.

Here are some excerpts from the *Selichos* for *Taanis Esther:*

> *Let my adversaries suffer for their malice, and let them be caught in the wiles which they deceitfully advised, saying, "The L-rd shall not see it, neither shall the G-d of Jacob regard it."*
>
> *For three days he (Mordechai) made the children suffer hunger and thirst, to weaken by the voice of Jacob the power of the insolent, and with outspread hands he prayed, "O L-rd, save me from ignominy, and let not the enemy come and slay mother and child!"*

Such prayers when recited with the proper fervor tend to attune the Jew to the inner spirit of the fast day, and at the same time prepare him for the joy of salvation commemorated in the festival of Purim.

A feature of the Jewish fast day which is not, usually, given proper attention is that of giving charity, in accordance with the maxim of the Rabbis that "the reward of the fast is the contribution of charity." Proper observance of this maxim is an excellent training for the child in the importance of *tzedakah*.

Purim

Though not containing the prohibitive elements of our *Yamim Tovim* — *Issur Melachah*, the prohibition of work — the festival of Purim is nevertheless rich in *Yom Tov* spirit. It is a day dedicated to joy without reservation, though the day itself remains a week day.

The festival is composed of various elements:

1. *Parsumei Nisa* — a public acclamation of the miracle of Purim — represented in the reading of the *Megillah betzibur* — publicly. During the reading of the *Megillah*, the Purim *gragger* becomes an important instrument of celebration. The *gragger* is not a mere noisemaker, and has no similarity to the secular tumult of a New Year's eve, which, by the way, has become quite an occasion for a good many Jews. The tumult in the synagogue upon the mention of Haman's name is a reaction against evil and its perpetrators. Here is an opportunity for the Jewish child to be trained into *Yiddishkeit* in a manner very close to his own heart. His natural inclination for noisemaking can be channeled into a vital lesson in *Yiddishkeit*. This is indicative of the attitude of the Jew, who sees in every human trait the possibility of serving G-d.

2. *Yom Mishteh V'simchah* — a day of feasting and rejoicing — this element of Purim is celebrated in the *Seudas Purim* — the Purim feast, which is eaten before sundown on Purim. The Purim *seudah* has always been an occasion for the Purim rhymes and "Purim Torah" — examples of true Jewish wit and humor, stemming from Torah and the deep wells of Jewish faith. The Purim *seudah* has many times been the setting of the Purim *shpiel* — the Purim play — where the Jew had occasion to give outlet to his talents for acting in a parody of the *golus* and his oppressors. The levity of Purim never became a raucous free-for-all. It was always tempered with the

knowledge that the levity was a form of *mitzvah* and, as such, part of the Jew's service to G-d. Only the Jew whose *simchah* is a *mitzvah* is capable of such forms of unrestrained restraint.

It is needless to say that the proper observance of this element of the festival can deeply impress the Jewish child with the idea that *mitzvos* embrace all facets of living — even levity can be channeled to the service of G-d. The *Seudas* Purim must therefore not be a haphazard affair, just another meal. It must be filled with the Purim spirit. Purim rhymes and Purim Torah taught to the child in school should be recited at the *seudah*. Purim songs, such as *Shoshanas Yaakov*, should be sung. Where it is possible to take advantage of a Purim *seudah* in a yeshivah, this should be done. The larger gathering is conducive to a fuller appreciation of the element of feasting and rejoicing.

3. *Mishloach Manos* — sending of gifts. The *Nes* Purim — the salvation of a great Jewish community from grave danger to their future survival — served to arouse a feeling of their common destiny as a people under the continuous guardianship of G-d. This feeling of common ties of brotherhood was given form in the *mitzvah* of sending gifts to one another on Purim. It is the result of the feeling of closeness brought on through the lesson of Purim and at the same time serves as cause to cement common ties of friendship.

Here again we are given an opportunity to give the sanctity of *mitzvah* to an act quite common in life. The sending of gifts on Purim, therefore, must be raised to the plane and level of sanctity. And when performed as the *mitzvah* requires, it strikes deep roots in the soil of the Jew. *Re'us* — bonds of friendship — when bound together with the ties of *mitzvos*, are more lasting and durable.

The parent should take time on Purim for the preparation of the gifts, consisting of food and drink, impressing upon the child the ceremonial of *mitzvah*. Let the child help in these preparations. Let him act as the *sheliach*, the messenger who delivers the gifts.

The child himself should be especially encouraged to

perform this *mitzvah*, among his own circle of friends, for this *mitzvah* deals with one of the basic elements in human society. In the life of the child, bonds of friendship are one of the great factors in his healthy spiritual development. In *Mishloach Manos* we have a *mitzvah* which tends to nurture this great factor in the molding of a happy and healthy personality.

4. *Matanos L'evyonim* — gifts to the poor and needy. In realizing our common destiny as a people we begin to feel our responsibility towards those of our brothers who are in need of our aid and help. We begin to feel that our sphere of interest in others embraces more than our family circle and friends.

The gifts on Purim also have the purpose of giving the poor and needy the possibility of enjoying the benefits of the festival of Purim themselves. It makes the festival all-inclusive.

An interesting feature of the *mitzvah* is the need of giving at least two gifts to each of two *evyonim* — poor people. The *mitzvah* thus becomes indicative of the donor's deeper interest in his brother; it is not merely the mechanical fulfillment of our obligation. The spirit of the *mitzvah* is such "that it is better to spend more in *matanos l'evyonim* than in the Purim *seudah* and *mishloach manos*, for there is no greater or more glorious joy than bringing happiness to the poor, the orphan and the widow. And in such manner a person likens himself to the *Shechinah* of Whom it is written, 'to raise the spirit of the lowly and the heart of the oppressed' " *(Rambam*, Hil. *Megillah* 2:17).

We cannot exaggerate the importance of training the child in this great *mitzvah*. In developing his personality as a Jew, this *mitzvah* is of prime importance. Encourage the child to take a few pennies from his weekly allowance to place into the various charity plates displayed in the synagogue on Purim. Let him be prepared prior to Purim so that he will need no prompting on Purim. We cannot overestimate the deep impression left on the child who feels that he has, on his own, participated in the observance of Purim, together with his elders, in the *mitzvah* of *matanos l'evyonim*.

The great lesson that Right conquers Might is taught in the

festival of Purim. G-d's providential guardianship of Israel at all times is evident in the miracle of Purim. In the very cycle of the natural course of events there is always present G-d's divine purpose. The sequence of events, though not understood at the time of their occurrence, ultimately reveals the handiwork of G-d.

It would be most advisable to discuss the eternal lesson of Purim at the Shabbos meal preceding Purim. Encourage the participation of the children in the discussion. It will be a spiritual adventure of great benefit both to the parent and the child. It will help a great deal in making the observance of the festival itself a spiritual experience of inestimable value.

Pesach

The spring season is heralded into Jewish life with the holiday of *Pesach*. At this season of the year, when nature begins to burst forth with new life, the Jew celebrates the birth of Israel as a nation. The soil of humanity, barren and arid of the Divine Word of G-d, became enriched and fructified with a new people whose very *raison d'être* was the permeation of mankind with Divinity — a *mamleches kohanim v'goi kadosh* — a kingdom of priests and a holy people.

No festival in Jewish life is so replete with the rich symbolism of *mitzvos* as the *Pesach* festival. And since *mitzvos* are the practical aspect of the depth of inspiration of the Jewish soul, Jewish parents should seek to make full use of the *Pesach* festival as a workshop in Jewish education, both for themselves and their children.

It was specifically of *Pesach* that the Rabbis spoke in teaching us — *sho'alim v'dorshim kodem ha'chag* — that one should acquaint himself prior to the festival with various elements of the holiday. One cannot possibly appreciate the Divine beauty of the *Pesach Yom Tov* without some previous preparation as to the laws and practices of the *Yom Tov*. The Jewish Day School gives the child a fair amount of preparation for the holiday, but it is the duty of the parent to translate the knowledge gained in school into the home atmosphere of the child. As part of this duty it is advisable that there be a discussion of the aspects of the *Yom Tov* between parent and child prior to the *Yom Tov*. This not only enhances for the child the importance of the knowledge gained in school, but it serves also to deepen the child's appreciation of the *Yom Tov*.

✺ Aspects of the Yom Tov

The holiday is known and designated by three names: *Chag Hamatzos*, the festival of matzos, *Chag Hapesach*, the festival of Passover, and *Z'man Cherusainu* — the time or season of our freedom.

Chag Hamatzos — this term reminds us both of the *mitzvah* of *matzoh* and the negative commandment to abstain from eating *chometz* (leaven) throughout the entire *Yom Tov*. Abstinence from *chometz* includes also the necessity of removing from one's possession any *chometz* which he may have. This necessitates a thorough cleaning of the house. And so spring cleaning for the Jew is an act of *mitzvah*, culminating in the *bedikas chometz* — the search for the *chometz* — on the evening preceding *Pesach*. And here we have a wonderful opportunity for the mother to train and educate her daughter in preparing for the *Yom Tov*. To make housecleaning a source of *Avodas Hashem* (Divine service) is yet another example of finding G-d in our most mundane affairs.

Bedikas Chometz should not be summarily done as something to get over with. This final act gives the halo of Divinity to the entire pre-*Pesach* preparation. It should therefore carry the solemnity of *mitzvah* called for in the recitation of the *b'rachah* preceding the *bedikah*. The children should participate in the search for *chometz* together with their father. There is something of mystery and adventure involved for the younger children. The children tense and excited, the *chometz* must be found. And when found, the reward is — a *mitzvah* performed!

The abstinence from *chometz* is the source for much of the special culinary art of the *Pesach* festival. Here again the mother has the opportunity of training her daughter in *mitzvos* through so simple a thing as the preparation of various Passover dishes.

◆§ The Seder

The festival of *Pesach* and *Z'man Cherusainu* receive their practical application in *mitzvah* at the *Seder* service. The *Seder* service, if properly performed, is beyond doubt one of the most beautiful and inspiring acts of *mitzvah* in all of Jewish life.

The *Seder* is essentially a workshop in Jewish education. It is centered in the commandment: *V'higad'to l'vincho bayom hahu* — and thou shalt relate unto thy children on that day (*Exodus* 13:8). The recitation of the *Haggadah* is really the lesson of *Pesach* in all its various facets being taught by the father to the child.

Since a basic element in education is arousing and maintaining the unabated interest of the child, the Rabbis instituted certain innovations in the *Seder* service with this program in mind. The *Ma Nishtanah* — the Four Questions asked by the child — is a direct result of this desire to have the child himself participate actively in the lesson of Passover.

This method of imparting knowledge in the form of an answer to a question is a valuable feature in education. Not only does it arouse interest; it also serves the purpose of better understanding the problem at hand. Asking a question calls for a certain degree of understanding. It gives one the opportunity to analyze and realize what he does know in order to seek information about that which he doesn't know. The Law, therefore, requires that even when there is no child present and all engaged in the *Seder* service are *talmidei chachomim*, it is still necessary that one of them ask the "four questions." And if one suffers the misfortune of having to perform the *Seder* service all alone, he must ask the four questions of himself (*Pesachim* 116a).

The *Arba Kosos* — the four cups of wine which we drink at the *Seder* — are indicative of four different terms used by the Torah in reference to Israel's salvation from Egyptian bondage.

Since the *Arba Kosos* commemorate Israel's freedom, they must be drunk in a manner befitting the free man and not a slave. Hence, the *Heseivah* — drinking while leaning on pillows, indicative of complete *cherus* (freedom). One of the four questions expresses the desire of the child to know the reason for this manifestation of *cherus*. In the recitation of the *Haggadah* the father informs the child of the great story of Israel's freedom through *Yetzias Mitzrayim*, the great lesson of G-d's rule over all forces of nature, and the concurrent lesson of Israel's role as the Chosen People.

Pride is infused into the child — pride with being a son of this Chosen People. *Emunah* (deep faith in G-d's Divine Providence) — Israel's wellspring of survival — is taught to the child. *Yiras Shomayim* (fear of the L-rd), Who is the Master of our destiny, is vividly presented in the glowing words of the *Haggadah*.

Maror (bitter herbs) reminds us of the affliction of the Jew, and *korech* (the sandwich of *matzah* and *maror)* reminds us of Israel's glorious past, when the sacrificial Paschal lamb was brought up in the Temple, and Jews ate matzah, *maror*, and the meat of the *korban Pesach.* This is something to fire the imagination of the child, to fill him with hope for final redemption, when once again we will be privileged to enjoy the Paschal Temple service.

The white robe — the *kittel* — worn by the father during the *Seder*, commemorating the Temple where such robes were worn (commentary, *Imrei Shefer*, Rabbi N.Z.Y. Berlin) serves to impress indelibly upon the child the memorable occasion of the *Seder* service.

Another *Seder* custom which serves to strengthen our *emunah* and our hope in final redemption is that of opening the door to admit Eliyahu Hanavi, who will bring us the tidings of salvation.

Participation in the *Seder* service with all its beauty and glory is an experience which leaves an everlasting impression upon the mind and heart of the Jew. There is no theatrical fanfare, but the results achieved are greater than that of any pageantry. What a sorrowful substitute for Torah beauty and glory are those "third *sedarim*" which many of our Jews have begun to hallow!

The *Seder* meal sandwiched in between the *Haggadah* and the *Hallel* is truly an act of Divine service. The spiritual elevation of the Jew imparts a different taste to the food. It was Rabbi Akiva who once told Tyranus Rufus of Rome that the *Shabbos* was the special spice which gave a unique taste to the *Shabbos* meal. The *Seder* service is the special spice of the *Seder* repast. And therefore, parents should take the trouble of maintaining the level of spiritual beauty during the meal. Passover songs are in order. *Divrei Torah* — discussing various phases of the *Haggadah* — are of greatest importance. The participation of the child is always to be remembered.

Sefiras Ha'omer

When the Temple was in existence an *omer* — a certain measure — of barley was brought as an offering upon the Altar. In conjunction with the bringing of the *Omer* we have been commanded to count seven weeks. This counting is to start on the second day of *Pesach* when the *Omer* was brought and ends with the celebration of the festival of *Shavuos*, which follows immediately after the culmination of the seven weeks.

This *mitzvah* indicates Israel's appreciation of the fact that true freedom is not that of the body but rather of the spirit. The Rabbis taught, "He is free who is engaged in the study of Torah." One of our great medieval authorities writes in reference to this *mitzvah*. "Receiving a Torah is of greater significance than freedom from bondage. We have therefore been commanded to count from the second day of *Pesach* until the day which commemorates the giving of the Torah, in order to demonstrate our deep desire for that day; just as the slave looks forward impatiently to his moment of freedom" (*Chinuch, mitzvah* 306). This *mitzvah* is therefore an integral part of the concept of *Z'man Cherusainu*. The parent should see to it that the child be careful in the observance of the *mitzvah.* He should be impressed with the deep lesson of the *mitzvah.* A discussion of this lesson at the second *Seder* would be most proper.

The period of *sefirah* is also one of national mourning and therefore no weddings or festivities are permitted during this period. Tradition tells us that during the period of *sefirah* the twenty-four thousand disciples of Rabbi Akiva died as a result of a plague which broke out.

No one can fail to overlook in this tradition the great lesson that the loss of great Torah scholars is a calamity of national magnitude. Since during the past year* we have had the great misfortune of losing two giants of the spirit, the saints and sages Chazon Ish and Rabbi Isser Zalman Meltzer, it would be fitting for the Jewish parent to impress the child with the national tragedy suffered in their loss. It is well for Jewish children to know that we possessed such great men. The story of their lives should be told to the child and he will appreciate something of the great loss which Israel has suffered in their passing. By the way, it is of great importance that the life stories of Israel's great spiritual luminaries become part of the reading material of the Jewish child.

Lag B'Omer

The thirty-third day of *sefirah* — the 18th day of Iyar — serves as a break in the period of mourning. It is a day for joyous occasions. The reason for this is that on *Lag B'Omer* the plague which destroyed so many of Rabbi Akiva's disciples came to a halt. Since the death of a *talmid chacham* is a national tragedy, then certainly his life is a cause for great rejoicing.

Lag B'Omer has always been a traditional holiday for Jewish schoolchildren. But little heed is paid to the cause for rejoicing.

---

* [Although this section of the present article first appeared in April of 1954, it is especially pertinent at the present time. Within less than a year we have been bereft of three Torah luminaries of our day, the Steipler Gaon, Rav Yaakov Kaminetsky, and Rav Moshe Feinstein, זצ״ל — M.G.]

In reality, the reason for the semi-holiday can become an incentive to the child to be a good pupil, to seek to excel in his Torah studies. For is it not the great gift of the life of a *talmid chacham* which is the very cause for rejoicing on *Lag B'Omer!*

Shavuos

The motif of the *Yom Tov*, as we know it today, is that of *Z'man Matan Toraseinu* — the festival commemorating the giving of the Torah on Sinai.

This motif of *Matan Torah* has no specific *mitzvah* attached to it. Torah is all-inclusive and cannot be limited to any special symbolism. *Ner mitzvah v'sorah or* — *mitzvah* is a lantern, Torah is light itself.

The quintessence of Torah is *Talmud Torah* — the study of Torah. Observance is void of content if it is not a direct result of the study of G-d's Holy Torah. And so it is customary to be up during the first night of the *Yom Tov* and to spend the entire night in Torah study. It is advisable that parents give their sons the opportunity of the thrill of this experience. Young children cannot be kept up for an entire night. But they should be taken to the *Beis Hamidrash* after the *Yom Tov* meal to spend some time in Torah study. The impression left by this spiritual adventure cannot be overestimated. Those who are privileged to live in a community blessed with a *yeshivah gedolah* should take advantage of *Shavuos* night at the yeshivah.

The importance of the lesson of *Shavuos* cannot however be impressed upon the child with this one night alone. A child must see a continual appreciation by his parents for Torah study. The parent should spend a certain portion of each day for Torah study in accordance with his abilities, whether it be the weekly portion of the Torah, *Shulchan Aruch, Mishnah* or *Gemara*. The Jewish home is pervaded with a completely different atmosphere where Torah is studied.

If a parent will realize what this means for the entire development of his child he will not seek excuses and alibis to free himself from this duty. It will be a labor of love, the most precious moments of his entire day. Many a child is a problem at school because he is disinterested in his studies. Little do parents realize how easily the malady could be remedied if they were to set an example for the child through their personal interest in Torah study.

Z'man Matan Toraseinu demands of us the setting of goals in the education of our children. A parent's entire outlook should be that of having his son become a *talmid chacham*, a proficient Torah scholar, well-versed in the great Torah heritage of Israel. The ignorance of Torah that prevails in Jewish life is, beyond doubt, the greatest source of all the evils and ills in the entire field of Jewish living. History has proven time and again that when Torah scholarship deteriorates Jewish life gradually loses its potency, until it is finally lost completely.

Torah scholarship does not end with the first seven grades of a Jewish Day School. It means *yeshivos gedolos* which carry on the tradition of Torah study as practiced through all ages of Jewish history. Torah scholarship cannot exist in an atmosphere of careerism. It grows in the soil of Jewish idealism which sees in the *Keser Torah* (crown of Torah) the greatest glory of life. It develops where there is a feeling that the true Jewish aristocrat is the *talmid chacham*. It calls for many years of devoted Torah study both by day and by night.

When parents, however, ask to what purpose is such study, a question which in simpler terms really amounts to asking what does it all mean in dollars and cents, the result is Jewish living as we know it in this country today. The ground becomes ripe for various movements and "philosophies" which speak in the name of Torah and tradition although completely void of and many times anti-Torah. In an atmosphere of *Am-aratzus* anything can be passed off as Torah and Jewish education. And beyond doubt, the *falsification* of Torah does more harm than the complete lack of Torah.

It is the binding duty of the Jewish parent to seek the proper perspective in Torah education. His duty to his child calls for deep work with himself. The proper approach of the parent himself to the entire problem of Jewish education is the best preparation for the child's observance of *Z'man Matan Toraseinu*.

The Jew's appreciation of the value of Torah finds expression in the *Shavuos* custom of eating *milchigs* (dairy), since Torah has been compared in various verses of the *Tanach* to milk, as in the verse of *Shir Hashirim* 4:11: *D'vash v'cholov tachas l'shoneich* — Honey and milk are under thy tongue. The spiritual nourishment of Torah has been compared to that of the fat of milk. The *Midrash* interprets this verse as referring to Torah study which should be as pleasant as the mixture of honey and milk (*Rabbah*, ad loc.). The dairy dishes on *Shavuos* are indicative, therefore, of the Jew's desire to make physical nourishment part of his spiritual experience. The Jewish daughter should help in preparation of these dishes as part of her *Yom Tov* experience.

Before the reading of the Torah on the first day of the *Yom Tov*, *Akdamus* is recited. This is a song of praise, composed in the eleventh century, dealing with the greatness of Torah, our everlasting love for it, and our determination to remain a people of Torah come what may. It would be well for both parents and child to become acquainted with the contents of this inspiring poem. Its recitation would then serve to enhance the celebration of this Torah *Yom Tov*.

The Three Weeks

There are days in Jewish life which commemorate national calamity and destruction. The great national calamity of *Churban Beis Hamikdash* is not something of Israel's past. The loss of the *Beis Hamikdash* as the central focal point of Jewish life is continually felt by the Jew and it is this great feeling and realization of loss which serves as the eternal source of hope for the rebuilding of Zion and Jerusalem.

Three weeks in the Jewish year have been set aside as a period of national mourning for the loss of the *Mikdash*. This period of mourning starts with the fast of *Shivah Asar B'Tammuz* and culminates in the fast of *Tishah B'Av*. The first fast commemorates the break in the wall of Jerusalem which enabled the enemy to enter the city, and the last fast commemorates the complete destruction of the *Beis Hamikdash*.

Since this period of mourning takes place after the close of the school year and usually when the child is away on vacation, the child is estranged from the great edifying effects of the "three weeks." The laws governing this period of mourning were made with a view towards deepening our appreciation of what our loss signifies for all of Jewish life.

Tishah B'Av, this great day of mourning, is nevertheless a day in which the prayer of *Tachanun* is not recited, for it has been called *moed* by the prophet — *Kora olai moed lishbor bachuroi*. The Almighty has designated the Ninth of Av as a day of destruction. *Designation* by the Almighty gives that day the specific quality of recognizing the manifestation of Divine Providence. *Hashem Yisborach* reveals Himself to us in the great national joy of *yetzias mitzraim* and in the great national sorrow of a *Tishah B'Av*. (I have heard this interpretation from my revered master, the great *gaon* Rav Avrohom Yitzchok Bloch, of sainted memory, Telzer Rov and Rosh Yeshivah.)

Certainly the activities and the environment of the Jewish child during this period of the year are not conducive to receiving the impressions of this great period of national mourning. Parents should give some thought to this matter and seek ways and means to rectify the situation. We deny our children a great factor in their proper growth and development as Jews when they do not feel the meaning of the "three weeks."

There can be no better means of developing a deep love and attachment to *Eretz Yisroel* than the proper observance of the three weeks. If the loss of a true *Eretz Yisroel* is a cause of deep national mourning then *Eretz Yisroel* must be a central factor in the entire framework of Jewish living.

Parents should certainly have their children participate in the *kinos* — lamentations of *Tishah B'Av*, recited in a darkened synagogue, whilst sitting on the floor before an *Aron Kodesh* unclothed of the splendor of its *paroches* — symbolic of Israel's loss of splendor. It is an experience which is bound to leave a great impression upon the child.

The great Zion songs at the end of the morning *kinos* are a great source of inspiration on the glory of Zion and Jerusalem. Both parent and child should be acquainted with their meaning.

The "three weeks" are followed by *Shabbos Nachmu* — the *Shabbos* on which the great words of consolation of the prophet Isaiah are read in the *Haftorah*. The Jew does not sink in despair but rather becomes uplifted to the great heights of Divine hope and comfort, filled with the conviction of Zion redeemed and Jerusalem rebuilt.

On War and Mobilization—
Zion and Jerusalem
The Nerve Center of the World

Hashem said through the Prophet Isaiah (62:1): "For the sake of Zion I will not hold My peace and for the sake of Jerusalem I will not be still."

The *Targum's* interpretation of this verse casts a brilliant light on the current world situation: Hashem pledges that until Zion and Jerusalem are peaceful and secure, He will allow no rest *to the nations of the earth.* The situation of the Jewish people cannot be viewed in a vacuum, separate and apart from the world order.

We are in the habit of scanning the long list of international crises and feeling that the situation of our beleaguered brothers in *Eretz Yisroel* would matter precious little to anyone except fellow Jews, were it not for the ever-present danger of a superpower confrontation. Energy crises, floundering Great Britain, Watergate and its threat to the American political system, French recalcitrance in Europe, Russo-Chinese hostility, the sanguinary "cease-fire" in Vietnam, and the list goes on and on. People who see things in "perspective" are well aware that

[The Yom Kippur War was a traumatic event in recent Jewish history. In this essay, adapted from *Shiur Daas* lectures to his students in the Telshe Yeshivah, the Rosh Yeshivah presents a Torah view of unfolding events. From *The Jewish Observer*, May, 1974. — Ed.]

in terms of "the big picture" a few pieces of real estate in Sinai and Golan are of little significance on the larger landscape. So on the one hand, we are grateful that the physical survival of three million Jews in Israel is interwoven in the fabric of American-Russian relations; hence, it is important enough to demand the notice of the White House and the Kremlin. But on the other hand, we tremble in anticipation of possible Jewish sacrifices upon the altar of detente and increased petroleum production.

Isaiah tells us we are wrong. *Eretz Yisroel* is not simply one problem in isolation of myriad world problems; it is a major source of world problems. Hashem has made a pledge that as long as Zion and Jerusalem live in crises and fear, the world will have no rest. Japan will falter and suffer loss of face. Great Britain will rock with domestic instability and a trade imbalance that boggles the mind. The United States will be told that it must curb its energy appetite and change its life-style. Why? Because the Supreme Being will allow rest and security to no nation as long as His most favored nation is threatened. It was no coincidence that Vietnam threatened to erupt again shortly after the Yom Kippur War, or that Europe, France and the United States descended to levels of petty squabbling unmatched since the trade wars of two generations ago; that political upheaval has threatened almost every major power these past months. Hashem will not be silent to others so long as they look with apathy or antipathy upon the tribulations of Zion and Jerusalem.

◄§ The Stakes are Even Higher

When we agonize over *Eretz Yisroel,* we are contemplating not only the Holy Land, but the entire universe, just as the heart surgeon knows that his area of specialization controls life itself.

Indeed, the stakes are even higher than that. The Prophetess Devorah curses those who did not come to the aid of her forces as they battled the hordes of Sisera "because they did not come to the help of the L-rd, to the help of the L-rd against the mighty men" (*Judges* 5:23). *Rashi* explains that whoever helps the Jews is as though he had helped G-d Himself. Our Sages comment on this same verse that whoever attacks the Jewish people wages war against the Creator, as it were; hence, whoever defends Jews, defends the Creator (*Sifri, Beha'aloscha*).

This, then, is the true perspective with which we must view not only the Yom Kippur War, but the entire pattern of world history. The Chofetz Chaim said when the Russo-Japanese War broke out, "This war is a message to Jews. We may not know what it is telling us, but there is no doubt that we must learn something from it, because *Chazal* taught us that "*ein puronius ba'ah le'olam ella bishvil Yisrael* — no world catastrophe strikes but for Israel." By the same token, whenever there is a major catastrophe in India, a bloodbath in Russia — we must always see in it a Divine message to Jews — a call for improvement and repentance. Surely when the cataclysmic events center on *Eretz Yisrael* itself, we must see in them a heavenly call.

In the immediate aftermath of the Yom Kippur War, there had been an uncontrollable tendency to sigh with relief — even to applaud a military victory that, in many ways, dwarfed the triumph of the Six Day War. This superficial reaction was quickly overtaken with grief and a wave of fault-fixing. Over two thousand lives were taken from a nation which has been taught since its inception that "saving a Jewish life is the equivalent of saving the whole world." The wounded number in the thousands — precious Jewish souls who will never see again, never walk again — whose bodies, sometimes even minds, will never be whole again. Sadat takes his losses with equanimity; he invests freely many thousands more to win the right to hold his head high. Lives may matter precious little to others; but for us, the loss of each of the twenty-five hundred is a catastrophe.

⋅๑ Catastrophe — A Rendezvous with G-d

We must be conditioned to see the Hand of G-d in all events — especially in catastrophe. — "He [G-d] has called an assembly *(moed)* against me to crush my young men" *(Eichah* 1:5), the Prophet Jeremiah laments. Because the verse describes *Tishah B'Av* as a *moed*, a term the Torah reserves for festivals — we do not say the *Tachanun* prayer on that day, as though it were indeed a festival! My Rebbe, the Telshe Rav זצ"ל, explains that this day of greatest national tragedy is indeed a *moed*, for the word refers to a time when G-d meets His people in a holy assembly, a time when we are privileged to see the Hand of *Hashem* ... We saw it when He redeemed us from *Mitzrayim*, and again when He gave us the Torah. And we saw it, too, when He rained destruction and suffering upon us on *Tishah B'Av*. The *churban Beis Hamikdash* was not the type of occurrence that could be likened to scores of other disasters that fill the pages of human history. It was obviously a heavenly act of retribution, the fulfillment of too many unheeded prophetic warnings. It was awesome and terrible. But it was still *moed*, an opportunity for the Jewish people to meet its Maker.

The Yom Kippur War, too, is a *moed* in its own way. *Hashem Yisborach* is calling us, making demands upon us. It is for us to decipher the message and act upon it.

⋅๑ For Whom the Rainbow?

Many are quick to blame the non-religious for all our woes. "Their sins caused the tragedy and still they refuse to learn their lesson from G-d's anger at them!" Let us stop looking at others and peer deep into ourselves. Let there be no mistake. The heavenly call comes not to non-believers; it is coming to those of the *Am Hashem* who know that our mission on earth is embodied in the Torah.

After the deluge, *Hashem* showed Noach the rainbow and told him that the rainbow would forever serve as a sign of the Divine covenant that such a flood would never again take place. The *Sforno* explains that from then on, the rainbow would be a heavenly sign to the righteous people that their generation has sinned and that it is their duty to teach and chastise their straying generation. He goes on to explain that when the righteous have perceived G-d's signal and done what is expected of them, G-d will take notice of the prayers of the righteous and withdraw His wrath from the human race.

Let us mark well the illuminating words of the *Sforno:* The heavenly call is to the *righteous of the generation* — not to the sinners. The sinners cannot hear the call; they look at the rainbow and see but a colorful spectrum. Their spiritual senses are deadened. But the righteous of the generation *can* hear and see; and they *can* interpret the heavenly sign. It is to them that G-d calls, and it is for them to respond by praying, coming closer to Torah, and trying to bring others along with them.

◦§ Bigger Things are Expected

This is not some abstract sort of obligation, a vague injunction to "do good and be good." *Hashem* expects us to strive for higher goals, and the penalties for not doing so can sometimes be enormous. King David once erred in ordering a census to be taken improperly. As a result, a plague broke out resulting in seventy thousand deaths (*I Samuel* 11:24). Our Sages explain the reason for so severe a punishment:

> *All seventy thousand men who died in the time of King David did so because they did not request the building of a Bais Hamikdash. If this was so serious a sin for them — people who never had a Bais Hamikdash, how much more so for us — who did have it and had it destroyed — if we do not beseech G-d in His mercy to rebuild it. Therefore, the righteous men of old established the blessing for the rebuilding of Jerusalem which is said three times daily in Shemoneh Esrei (Midrash Tehillim 17).*

Obviously, bigger things are expected of us than we sometimes are willing to acknowledge. It is not sufficient to go about our everyday affairs even when they include performance of *mitzvos* and study of Torah. Business as usual might be adequate in usual times, but these are not ordinary times for the Jewish people. If we were deluded into thinking so before, we surely cannot go on thinking so in the wake of the Yom Kippur War. Now, more than ever, is the time to heed the heavenly signs that demand of us that we shake ourselves loose from our lethargy and exert maximum efforts to strengthen our commitment to Torah. If, at a time like this, we persist in counting Phantoms, discussing the tactics and motives of Dr. Kissinger, and pin our hopes on the survival in office and the continued initiatives of President Nixon, then we are clearly conveying a lack of comprehension of the Divine message.

◈ Retreat to Life

A mishnah in the Tractate *Keilim*, chapter 17, says: "All items made from fish and other sea life cannot be rendered ritually impure"; the Torah ordains that only land animals and fowl are subject to impurity. "There is one exception to this rule," the mishnah continues. "It is *kelev sheba'yam* — a sea lion." Why is the sea lion different? Because when it is in danger, it flees to dry land — proving that, despite its habitation of the seas, it is basically a land animal.

Reb Tzadok Hakohen of Lublin draws an incisive moral lesson from this mishnah. If we want to determine someone's true character, we must observe him in time of crisis. People may preach loyalty to Torah and absolute belief in Hashem, but even they cannot know how sincere their preachments are until they are challenged by events. What happens to the honesty of a businessman if he perceives truth as costing him dearly ... does he put Torah imperatives above expediency and profit? What happens to the faith of the observant Jew when a dear one is deathly ill — does he hang only onto his doctor's word, or does he know that his *Tehillim* is more potent than a prescription pad? And where was each of us when our brothers and sisters in *Eretz Yisroel* were in mortal danger — and where are we now when the danger is less obvious, but still present? It is now that we are being tested. These are the times when we can turn the tide by extra hours of Torah study, extra *tefillah* and extra *tzedakah*, a deeper commitment to a Torah way of life.

The signs have been given to us. Reliance on the morality of statesmen, on international law, on the United States have all been shown to be the slenderest of reeds. We are in the most precarious of bargaining positions by all the accepted laws of politics. The Zionist dream of a nation like all nations has been forever shattered; Israel has become a client state of the United States and it will take nothing more than a withdrawal of the American defense commitment to bring the Arab hordes in for the final kill. "— Who can predict how another American administration will define its foreign policy objectives, or what uncertain gasoline supplies and ballooning prices will do to American public opinion? There is already increasing support for the "rights of the Palestinians"; and the Arab states are only beginning to learn how to exploit the techniques of the sophisticated, civilized public relations, winning support from the man in the street.

The frightening list can be continued, but the point should already be clear. Whatever other lessons the Yom Kippur War may hold, it certainly cries out to us that we are a people in danger and that we must choose our refuge. If we expect to find it by seeing what the political pundits have to say, where the Gallup Polls point, what Dr. Kissinger is saying between the lines, and so on, then we are demonstrating that, when the chips are down, we are as secular and materialistic as those whom we so often decry. If, on the other hand, we turn to the *Bais Hamidrash* and *Bais Haknesses* when we are endangered, then we are showing that we are truly worthy of being called the nation of Hashem.

As the *Sforno* points out in his commentary on Noach's rainbow, the heavenly sign is not a call to the broad, unseeing masses of humanity. Rather, it is directed specifically toward those who are capable of seeing, understanding, and acting upon it. We have no right to let ourselves be swept away by waves of media reportage on the superficialities of war and survival. Its true story will not be formed in yesterday's military strategy (the Bar Lev Line was weak, the Arabs failed to win because they employed classic Russian tank strategy, and so on, ad infinitum) or tomorrow's negotiating ploys in Geneva. Its true story was written millennia ago in the Scriptures and Talmud. Victory and defeat are in the Hands of G-d, and we can direct those Hands by our Torah and *tefillah.*

⋖§ Heeding Devorah's Call

When we look at a faraway war through Torah binoculars, then it truly becomes part of an immediate experience. Every one of us has the responsibility to be at the front in the Torah's terms. Devorah the Prophetess mercilessly castigated those tribes and individuals who did not come to help. *Where was Reuven? ... why did Dan remain by its ships? Asher stayed by its safe seashore ... Mairoz is accursed ... There was a mobilization and they were found wanting ... for their reticence there is no forgiveness. Their people needed them, but they didn't come.* Devorah, mother of her people, can find no justification for her wayward children.

But there were others who likewise were not to be found in the infantry. For them, Devorah had only praise, because they joined the battle in their own way, in an enormously significant way. "My heart goes out to the lawgivers of Israel," she said, "that offered themselves willingly among the people, Bless the L-rd!" The *Targum* beautifully illuminates her gratitude to the lawgivers: Devorah said that she was G-d's agent to praise the Torah sages. During the years of alien oppression, they never stopped teaching the Torah, so it is fitting that they should now sit in the place of honor in the study halls expounding the Torah, blessing and thanking G-d. They sacrificed their personal interests to go about the land, teaching, and joining to form courts when the law had to be decided *(Shoftim* 5:9,10).

Her words are directed at our generation as much as her own. When Jews are in danger, the mobilization must be complete, all inclusive. Everyone who *can* help, *must* help. But ultimately, the forces of evil are attacking G-d Himself when they bare their fangs at Israel. In a battle against G-d, our most powerful weapons are Torah and *mitzvos*. The Sages who ignored odds, public opinion, and inconvenience to study and spread Torah were also part of the army; and Devorah, who knew the reasons for her miraculous victory, gave her heart to them.

We must learn this from the current war, for we failed to learn it from the 1967 War. The cacophony of pronouncements, threats, and soothing statements that fill the airwaves and the newspapers should not deter us from hearing and seeing the truth. The world will continue to be turbulent as long as *Eretz Yisroel* is threatened, and *Eretz Yisroel* will continue to be menaced until every single one of us heeds the call to mobilize in the only meaningful way.

A Path Through the Ashes:

Some Thoughts on Teaching the Holocaust

Precepts of Jewish thought are closely tied to everyday realities. The individual Jew can strengthen his *emunah* and *bitachon* (belief and trust in G-d) through the daily occurrences that befall him. Primary means for the transmission of fundamental principles in *emunah*, however, have been left undeveloped. Jewish history is such an uncharted field. Secular sources have been permitted to tread this land with familiarity and to interpret it with an assumed authority from their own perspective, while we have defaulted. We read their writings, accept their "facts," and in the process unconsciously become products of their outlooks. It is precisely in this field of Jewish history that a non-Torah orientation can be the most detrimental to Jewish thought.

We do, indeed, have an approach of our own: In *Parshas Ha'azinu*, the Torah gives us guidelines for the viewing and understanding of history from a true perspective: זְכֹר יְמוֹת עוֹלָם בִּינוּ שְׁנוֹת דֹּר וָדֹר, *Remember days of yore, understand the years of every generation (Devarim 32:7)*. If one wishes to

---

[No event of our century is more traumatic or more difficult to teach than the Holocaust. In this essay, adapted from an enthusiastically received address to a Torah Umesorah Teachers Conference, the Rosh Yeshivah gives profound and inspiring answers. From *The Jewish Observer, June, 1974.* — Ed.]

comprehend an event in history, one cannot look at it in the limited scope of the finite here and now; rather, one must understand the event as having a place in the historical continuum. A historical occurrence extends itself beyond the isolation of time and space, and reaches towards the past and the future, to acquire true significance. But one must invariably begin with Creation and the Creator. As the *Vilna Gaon* explained, to understand "the years of every generation," one must first "remember the days of yore" — the Six Days of Creation. For in those days lies the complete plan of the development of the universe and humankind in it. This, the *Gaon* taught, is the only way to understand history.

Secular sources view history in perspectives of their own, predicated on economic, social, and political principles. By contrast, the Torah directs us to view history as the unfolding of the Divine plan. History is the metamorphosis of man through the stages of destruction and redemption, continuing toward his final redemption in the days of *Moshiach.* And all such events, the redemptions and the destructions, are perceived as fundamental testimony to the presence of G-d in this world, and are understood as experiential units in *hashgachah pratis*, the active force of the Hand of G-d.

◆§ Children of the Holocaust

Redemption and destruction — familiar themes in Jewish history, and we, too, know them well. We, today, are all children of the Holocaust. Some have lived through it and some were born afterward. But all of us are deeply affected by it. Yet, the Holocaust has been left untapped as a resource in the teaching and imbuing of *emunah* in the hearts of those who came after it.

We are one generation removed, and this awesome occurrence somehow slipped out of the consciousness of most people. People forget, either due to preoccupation with daily matters, or because of inability to view the Holocaust in its true perspective and to reconcile it within themselves.

We are late in dealing with the Holocaust. *Chazal* explain the corrosive effect time has on the experiential quality of an occurrence. A *midrash* on *Megillas Eichah* (the Prophet Jeremiah's Lamentations on the destruction of the *Beis Hamikdash*) comments on the verse: *Hashem destroyed without mercy. Chazal* say that a hundred years after the *Churban* (destruction of the Second *Beis Hamikdash*), Rabbi Yochanan was able to explain this verse in sixty different ways, whereas *Rabbeinu Hakadosh* R' Yehudah HaNasi who lived one generation before him, was able to explain it in twenty-four ways. The Sages tell us that because *Rabbeinu Hakadosh* was one generation closer to the *Churban*, even though he did not live in the time of the *Churban* itself, he and his colleagues felt the intensity of the lamentation and the sorrow that much more deeply. After explaining the *pasuk* in twenty-four different ways, he would break down and weep. He did not have the emotional stamina to continue. Rabbi Yochanan and his companions, who lived one generation later, were that much more removed from the *Churban* and could therefore deal with it at greater length.

We are only one generation removed from the *Churban* of European Jewry, and yet the memory fades from our minds. Our emotional bankruptcy permits us to speak about it casually, in a detached manner, and even forget about it.

◄§ The "Churban" Fountainhead

We cannot permit the *Churban*, which has destroyed so many of our people and so much of our spiritual life, to pass into oblivion. We must reach out to it and grasp it before too much time elapses. Every detail is, of course, of utmost importance. But first, we must approach the entire concept of *Churban* at its harshest, and attempt to determine what it signifies in our relationship with G-d.

Truly understanding this most recent *Churban* does not begin with a particular event of a generation ago. It must begin with works written 2,500 years ago. Jeremiah the Prophet had written *"Hashem destroyed without mercy,"* regarding the destruction of the First *Beis Hamikdash*. Yet, this *pasuk* has been understood to extend beyond that *Churban* to include *Churban* in all times. The *Churban* of the *Beis Hamikdash* becomes the paradigm for all future *Churbanos*, and the Lamentations which the Prophet wrote with Divine inspiration encompass all sorrow, pain and mourning. All cries of loss and despair are united: *Chazal* interpret Jeremiah's outcry of עַל אֵלֶּה אֲנִי בוֹכִיָה — *For these do I weep*," as referring to events that occurred during the destruction of the Second Temple, even though the Prophet lived at the time of the First Temple ... we lack the power to make *kinos* (lamentations) of our own, so our lamentations find voice through the words of the *Navi*. His words are a vehicle for us to view and to understand the events of our time in the broad historical continuum, through an *emunah* perspective.

When referring to *Tishah B'Av* (the day the Temple was destroyed) the Prophet Jeremiah calls the day *moed*, a word that usually refers to a festival. The Telshe Rav, Horav Reb Avraham Yitzchak Bloch, explains that the word *moed* (מועד) is derived from the word *vaad* (ועד), appointment. It is a time of appointment of *Hashem* with the world, when His greatness is manifested. This greatness can be seen from two aspects: through the miracles of redemption, joy and happiness — the exodus from Egypt; or through destruction, pain and sorrow — the exodus from Jerusalem, a destruction so great that it could only have been administered by Divine plan ... two separate moments in the history of *Klal Yisrael: Geulah* and *Churban*, redemption and destruction. From the time the Second Temple was destroyed through the present, and on until the final redemption, we are caught in one long moment of "going out of Jerusalem," punctuated by especially harrowing experiences, such as the Holocaust.

◄§ "Churban" as a Father's Punishment

How does one approach these moments of anguish in the history of the Jewish People? What brings about this destruction? The *Navi* explains that the exile from Jerusalem is a result of sin, in a relationship of crime and subsequent